illustrations
and text by
John Minnion

contributing editor
Sonja Wirwohl
edited by
Jacqueline Krendel

HITLER'S LIST

an
illustrated
guide to
'degenerates'
jews
bolshevists
and other
undesirable
geniuses

**Checkmate
Books** Ltd

INTRODUCTION

Caricature has usually been seen as a weapon: more waspsting than bayonet perhaps, but nasty enough to prick a swollen ego. In the Third Reich, caricaturists played their poisonous part in the campaign against the Jews, imprinting on German minds a visual stereotype of swarthy, hook-nosed clutchers of moneybags.

The pictures in this book, whether you call them caricatures or portraits, were drawn out of respect and sympathy for their subjects. These are all remarkable people; not saints perhaps (apart from one), but individuals who have given much to, and in some cases transformed, our culture. Their lives deserve celebration.

In the darkest hours of the 20th century, some of the most highly civilised areas of Europe were highjacked by an ideology that defined these people and their work as 'degenerate'. One label that damned them was 'bolshevist': Hitler knew Communism to be his most organised enemy. But the accusation most damning of all was to be called 'Jewish' – even if you were not – and it was a label that encompassed a whole lot more than ethnic definition: modernism, abstract art, atonal music and theoretical physics (such as quantum theory) were all condemned as 'Jewish'; and so was jazz, pychoanalysis and even gothic type (*see* right).

Those individuals who actually were Jewish by birth were, on the whole, assimilated into German society, their Jewishness something that they thought very little about – until Hitler's malign plans took root. Many such 'undesirables' tried to get out of Nazi Germany if they could. Some didn't make it, or chose the wrong havens – countries that Hitler subsequently invaded. Some took their own lives. Others did escape, both Jews and non-Jews, and survived considerable trauma to enrich the culture of our times. Their accumulated stories make up this book. *John Minnion*

𝕭ndesirable typefaces

THIS BOOK IS SET almost entirely in Futura, a geometrically based font designed in 1927 by Paul Renner (*see* p.82). The Nazis rejected such modernist, sanserif typefaces as 'cultural bolshevism'. But they also rejected roman serif types as being 'un-German'. Instead they insisted that gothic script, particularly **𝕱raktur**, was the true script of the German *Volk* (people), unchanged since the Nuremberg Court of the 16th century. Renner compared Fraktur to lederhosen: a leftover from the past, now quaint.

Then, out of the blue in January 1941, came a Nazi decree describing gothic script as a 'Jewish abomination' that had infiltrated the culture due to Jewish ownership of printing presses. This apparently ludicrous turnaround disguised a practicality: Germany was now imposing its world order on conquered countries, and the natives just couldn't read gothic type.

So **gothic** had to go, and there was no clean alternative. Not for the last time, the Nazis had backed themselves into an ideological cul-de-sac.

HITLER'S LIST

an illustrated

guide to

'degenerates'

jews

bolshevists

and other

undesirable

geniuses

First published in Great Britain in 2004
as a numbered edition of 1000
by Checkmate Books Ltd
in association with the Galicia Jewish Museum, Poland

This revised edition published in 2005 by

Checkmate Books Ltd

65 Dudlow Lane
Liverpool L18 2EY England
Telephone +44 (0)151-722 8950
E-mail contact@checkmatebooks.com
www.checkmatebooks.com

Re-use of pictures

Enquiries should be made to
contact@checkmatebooks.com

ISBN 0–9544499–3–2

Printed by Page Bros (Norwich) Ltd

To Sandra

CONTENTS

1

Undesirable

philoso|

NIETZSCHE

phy

In a Bavarian prison cell, 35-year-old convict Adolf Hitler was beginning a five-year sentence for treason, after attempting to overthrow the German government. He was a celebrity prisoner, esteemed and venerated by his gaolers and fellow convicts. In a letter recommending early release, the prison governor called him 'amenable, unassuming and modest'. He 'never made exceptional demands' (perhaps because of the exceptional privileges he was given) and had 'no personal vanity'. He occupied his time pacing his commodious cell and dictating a best-selling autobiography to his fellow prisoner Rudolf Hess.

It was 1924: Germany had staggered giddily out of a roller-coaster year of extreme hyperinflation when mounds of useless billion-mark notes lay discarded by hungry workers, and trading had simply collapsed. The crisis had eased, but who knew what might happen next? The Weimar Republic, set up in the aftermath of the World War I defeat, was politically fragile, forever wrestling with the infernal triangle of unemployment, inflation and the reparation requirements made in the Versailles Treaty. There were rumours: Communists taking over Saxony; revolutionary garrisons marching on Berlin; the Rhineland seceding, the Kaiser returning; new-formed political leagues, of left and right, organising rifle-training sessions in the woods. And messiahs, preaching extreme roads to salvation – Hitler was just one of these.

By Christmas he was a free man, back in command of the National Socialists (Nazis) and beginning to be a force to be reckoned with. He continued to dictate his memoirs (he was a great dictator) and *Mein Kampf* was published in 1927. *My Struggle* (his working title had been more of a rant than that) brooded over Germany's suffering at the unjustness of the Versailles Treaty, diagnosed the national malady as a deep-rooted 'degeneracy' and outlined his plan for a cure: a great cleansing to rid the culture of the 'degenerate' elements. These pollutants were crystal-clear to him: Communists; Jews. Anyone who stood in the way of making Germany a racially pure, politically uniform *Volk*. And, he demanded, this cleansing of the culture must be extended to all fields. Theatre, art, literature, music, science, cinema, posters and window-displays 'must be purged of all manifestations of our rotting world and placed in the service of a moral, political and cultural idea'.

In the next few years, the so-called 'quiet years' of Nazi history, the National Socialist Party grew and Hitler's ideology found fertile soil and flourished.

Hitler's imagination was greatly stimulated by the philosopher Friedrich Nietzsche. Though he was not a fellow anti-Semite, Nietzsche (1844–1900) proclaimed the coming of the Master Race, the Superman: a 'magnificent blond brute, avidly rampant for spoil and victory'. Society, he said, 'is not entitled to exist for its own sake, but only as a substructure and scaffolding by means of which a select race of beings may elevate themselves to their higher duties'. He talked of a time when 'the strong men, the masters, regain the pure conscience of a beast of prey; monsters filled with joy'. Hitler loved phrases like that.

There were, of course, other influential philosophers and other, very different – but no less profound – ideas circulating in Germany and Austria at this time. However, many of the greatest minds were Jewish, and therefore, in Hitler's eyes, degenerate. The events that he was about to unleash were to give these thinkers enough to reflect on for the rest of the century.

KARL POPPER

born Vienna
Austria
1902
died Croydon
England
1994

POPPER BY NAME, popper by trade: he was always asking questions. In 1946 he addressed the Cambridge Moral Science Club with the question 'Are there any philosophical problems?' and provoked Wittgenstein, who believed there were only linguistic puzzles, to brandish a poker at him. Believing that 'great men may make great mistakes', he became a philosophical giant partly by being a giant-slayer, riding roughshod over any number of 'isms', especially historicism, probabilism and logical positivism. He attacked Plato for his utopian wish to arrest all political change, and Marx and Freud for theories which, he argued, were non-scientific because they were not open to falsifiability. Briefly a Marxist himself, he quickly came to despise the Fascist and Communist belief in inexorable laws of historical destiny. To Popper, Hitler's

vision of destiny, his ideal society that must first be purged of degeneracy, echoed the errors of Plato's utopian *Republic*. To create an uncorrupted state, Plato had advocated expelling everyone over the age of ten, and 're-educating' the children.

A Viennese schoolteacher whose first love was music, Popper adored Bach and loathed Wagner, considering Schubert the last great composer. He particularly detested Wagner's self-assessment as a genius 'ahead of his time', as if music inevitably transcended itself. This idea he scorned as 'historicism', and preferred to equate a great piece of music with a great scientific theory: 'a cosmos imposed on chaos'.

He anticipated the Nazi annexation of Austria and knew his Jewish ancestry would condemn him (though his family were in fact Lutherans). He took a lecturing job in New Zealand, then moved to England, where he taught for 24 years at the London School of Economics.

The Poverty of Historicism (1957) and ***The Open Society and its Enemies*** (1945) were Popper's most impassioned and influential books, powerful critiques of the philosophical thinking behind all forms of totalitarianism. Only an 'open society', which accepts changes and adapts, is a civilised and sustainable society. Despite the comfort in the idea of a fixed vision, we must, he says, bear the insecurity of social change, the 'strain of civilisation'. It is 'the price to be paid for every increase in our knowledge, in reasonableness, in co-operation, and in mutual help, and consequently, in our chances of survival'.

"I personally call the type of government which can be removed without violence 'democracy', and the other, 'tyranny'**"**

3

HANNAH ARENDT

born Hanover
Germany
1906
died New York
USA
1975

UNORTHODOX, CONTROVERSIAL, provocative; one of the most influential political thinkers of the 20th century, who explored on a grand scale the issues of her time, in books such as **The Human Condition** and **The Life of the Mind**.

As an 18-year-old theology student at Marburg she started a passionate affair with her professor, the phenomenological philosopher Martin Heidegger, a mentoring relationship which was renewed many years later, despite Heidegger's Nazi and anti-Semitic activities during the intervening years. Her loyalty to his person — she once compared him to Thales the Greek philosopher, who while gazing at the stars fell into a well — sits ambiguously alongside her life's work which regularly addressed the dilemma of her fellow German Jews. The rise of Nazism made her a political activist: she was jailed by the Gestapo for researching anti-Semitic propaganda, but released when a prison guard felt sympathy towards her. She fled to Paris and involved herself in the rescue of Jewish children from the Third Reich, bringing them to safety in Palestine. When the Nazis invaded France, she was imprisoned, but escaped and reached America in 1941.

There she quickly established a reputation as an intellectual, publishing her most influential book **The Origins of Totalitarianism** in 1951. She covered the trial of the Nazi war criminal Adolf Eichmann for the *New Yorker*, and wrote **Eichmann in Jerusalem**, in which she talked of the 'banality of evil'. Without taking his side in any way or doubting his guilt, she argued that Eichmann was a bureaucrat who believed that following orders and doing his duty absolved him from accountability for his own deeds. To Arendt, this was his 'horrible gift for consoling himself with clichés'; his sin, she said, was 'thoughtlessness'. Her overriding question was whether 'the act of thinking as such … could make men abstain from evil-doing or even actually condition them against it'. To some, this was too flat a response to the monstrousness of his crime and tantamount to excusing him. She was perceived as lacking compassion for the victims and, furthermore, betraying her people. But it mattered very much to her that her Jewishness should not be a factor in her judgement. She argued that the personal should never be political, that a person's 'political space' should be protected from private emotions and sentimentality — which included the love of one's people. 'The only love I know of and believe in is the love of persons.'

"Evil is never radical, only extreme; it possesses neither depth nor any demonic dimension. It can overgrow and lay waste the whole world precisely because it spreads like a fungus on the surface. That is its banality"

The Human Condition.

JOHN
MINNION·03

5

LUDWIG WITTGENSTEIN

born Vienna

Austria

1889

died Cambridge

England

1951

'I DID MEET ONE JEWISH BOY who was treated by all of us with caution,' confessed Hitler in *Mein Kampf*. There are some who say this boy was Wittgenstein, and that this very mild expression of distaste for a fellow schoolboy conceals a rabid personal hatred, the germ from which Hitler's anti-Semitism — and all that came from it — developed. This would make Wittgenstein number one on Hitler's List … assuming it were true. He *was* at school with Hitler, but (though six days younger) was two years above him, and one of 15 or so Jews. Although they had aloofness in common, and the tendency to whistle long passages of Wagner, there is no real evidence they even knew each other.

Nevertheless, Wittgenstein did come from just the sort of rich, cultivated, upper-class, Aryanised Jewish family that Hitler fulminated against as he wandered the streets of Vienna, and vilified in *Mein Kampf*. In contrast

to Hitler's father (a lowly functionary), Ludwig's father owned large slices of Austria's iron and steel, railway and tyre industries.

Smarting from his rejections from the Vienna Art Academy, Hitler came to view himself as an outcast in his own country because of Jews, and he began to see them everywhere, like invading Martians: 'In the course of the centuries their outward appearance had become Europeanised and had taken on a human look; in fact, I even took them for Germans.' He looked for, and found, Jewish names behind everything he considered unclean in public artistic life, in politics and the press. 'Was there any form of filth or profligacy, particularly in cultural life, without at least one Jew involved in it?'

Yet someone like Wittgenstein hardly considered himself a Jew at all. The youngest of eight, he grew up thinking his father to be a Protestant and his mother a Catholic. It was lucky he was abroad when Hitler took over Austria. His family remained, but were safe only because they paid the Nazis large sums to grant them 'half-breed' status.

The Wittgensteins were intellectual and musical: Mahler and Brahms were house-visitors, and one of Ludwig's brothers, Paul, was the one-armed pianist for whom Ravel wrote his first piano concerto. The other three brothers committed suicide. Ludwig, too, was somewhat heedless of his own mortality — it won him medals for bravery in World War I. He had extreme

"Nothing is so difficult as not deceiving yourself"

intellectual intensity and an obsession with moral and philosophical perfection, as well as mechanical ability: he studied engineering in Berlin and Manchester, researching the movements of kites and designing an aeronautical engine. In Cambridge, he became a student of the philosopher Bertrand Russell, who said he had 'fire and penetration and intellectual purity to a quite extraordinary degree ... [He] soon knew all that I had to teach'. 1918 found him in an Italian prisoner-of-war camp, from which his manuscript for ***Tractatus Logico-Philosophicus*** – the only work to appear in print in his lifetime – was smuggled out to Russell, who managed with some difficulty to get it published. In the words of British philosopher Bryan Magee, it 'maintained that almost everything that is most important cannot be stated at all but only, at the very best, indicated by our use of language'.

Temporarily assuming that this work had solved all solvable questions regarding logic, Wittgenstein abandoned philosophy and gave away the family fortune (his father had astutely invested in American bonds) to writers and artists such as Rainer Maria Rilke. He became first a primary school teacher, then a monastery gardener. After that, pausing only to design and build a house for his sister, he returned to Cambridge and became Professor of Philosophy. For much of World War II he was a porter at Guy's Hospital. His final years were spent working in seclusion on the west coast of Ireland. And his last words were, 'Tell them I've had a wonderful life.'

7

THEODOR W. ADORNO

born Frankfurt
Germany
1903
died Visp
Switzerland
1969

A BUSY MAN, multi-talented, intellectual; a pianist, composer and musicologist, who studied philosophy, sociology, psychology and music at Frankfurt University and then composition with Alban Berg in Vienna. In Nazi eyes he was both Jewish and bolshevist, though only his father had Jewish blood. He was forced out of his philosophy lectureship in 1933 and left for Oxford, then the USA. He then adopted his mother's surname, relegating the Jewish-sounding Wiesengrund to a middle initial.

Adorno was an influence on all around him, whether persuading Solti to conduct Mahler, co-writing a guide to film music with Eisler, or muscling in on Thomas Mann's novel *Doctor Faustus*. He was a key member of the Institute for Social Research, known as the Frankfurt School, along with Walter Benjamin and Max Horkheimer. With the latter, he wrote **The Dialectic of Enlightenment** (1947) which addressed the rise of Nazism by asking why the supposedly 'enlightened' world was sinking into barbarism, concluding that not a lack of reason, but the very rationalisation of human society had ultimately led to Fascism. This book also contained the prescient essay **The Culture Industry: Enlightenment As Mass Deception**, which argues that within capitalist society, popular culture and shallow, easily digested products are used to pacify the masses and keep them apathetic. The 'culture industry', he said, creates false needs, thus turning the commodity into a fetish. He pinpointed television as 'derisively fulfilling the Wagnerian dream of ... the fusion of all the arts in one work'. TV, he wrote, 'promises drastic impoverishment of aesthetic matter'. He also predicted the contrived catharsis of talk shows and the dissolving distinction between advertising and entertainment. 'The culture industry intentionally integrates its consumers from above,' he said, adding that he had preferred that term to 'mass culture' because the latter implied having arisen spontaneously from the masses themselves.

He returned to Frankfurt in 1949, re-established the Frankfurt School, and started lecturing again. In 1950, he published **The Authoritarian Personality** about the personal traits that, en masse, lead to totalitarianism: rigid, stereotyped ideas of normality; submission to authority; intolerance of ambiguity; insecurity and anxiety in the face of events that upset a world view; absolute ideas of right and wrong — these are all marks of an authoritarian personality. And, of course, were universal amongst the Nazis.

"For a man who no longer has a homeland, writing becomes a place to live"

8

9

WALTER BENJAMIN

born Berlin
Germany
1892
died Port-Bau
Spain
1940

'PROBABLY THE MOST PECULIAR Marxist ever,' said Hannah Arendt about this writer, philosopher, critic, translator and bibliophile. His interests in psychoanalysis, surrealism and messianic Judaic theology ensured that he could never be a routine Communist. He was, though, interested enough to visit Moscow in 1926 when he observed that the proletariat had 'confidently taken possession of the bourgeois culture'. The son of a Jewish antiques dealer, he studied philosophy, German and art history, though his thesis **The Origins of the German Tragedy**, with which he hoped to secure a professorship at Frankfurt, was rejected, not because of the contents but due to his 'unconventional lifestyle'. At a time when such things were marginal and exotic, he wrote an essay on **Hashish in Marseilles**, intending to follow it with a bigger study based on his personal experiments with mescaline and opium. He worked in poverty as a free-lance critic and author, first in Berlin — where his friends included Adorno, Brecht and Weill — and then in Paris, after emigrating in 1933. He published his most renowned essay **The Work of Art in the Age of Mechanical Reproduction** in 1936, elucidating how the reproducibility of original works of art leads to the loss of the *aura* of the work, and, while making art more democratic, reduces its authority as an object.

One work of art that had significant aura for Benjamin was a Paul Klee watercolour, *Angelus Novus*, which he bought in 1921 for 1000 marks (not so much at that time). From contemplation of the angelic figure — which seems suspended in time and space and about to be blown backwards — he conceived a profound image of the 'angel of history'. 'His face is turned towards the past. Where we perceive a chain of events, he sees one single catastrophe which keeps piling wreckage upon wreckage and hurls it in front of his feet. The angel would like to stay, awaken the dead, and make whole what has been smashed.' But a celestial wind rushes him backwards into the future.

As a German living in France, he was interned at the outbreak of war, then released thanks to friends. When the Germans invaded, he abandoned Paris in a rush, leaving many manuscripts behind. With a US visa in his pocket he made it to the Pyrenees, but was thwarted by Spanish guards. In fear of being turned over to the Gestapo, who were well aware that he was both Jewish and a Marxist, he took his own life with an overdose of morphine. Most of his work was published posthumously, most recently (1982) the **Arcades Project**, a remarkable 900-page patchwork of quotations and commentaries about the shopping arcades of 19th-century Paris.

"Fascism is the aestheticisation of politics**"**

1918
- End of World War I

1919
- Treaty of Versailles
- Weimar Republic established

1920
- Nazi Party established

1921
- SA (storm troopers) established

1923
- Hitler's 'Beer Hall' putsch fails to overthrow government

1924
- Hitler imprisoned, starts to write *Mein Kampf*. Freed by Christmas
- May Reichstag elections: Nazis win 6.6% of vote
- December Reichstag elections: Nazis win 3% of vote

1928
- May Reichstag elections: Nazis win 2.6% of vote

1929
- Great Depression begins

1930
- September Reichstag elections: Nazis win 18.3% of vote

1932
- July Reichstag elections: Nazis win 37.4% of vote
- November Reichstag elections: Nazis win 33% of vote

MARTIN BUBER

born Vienna
Austria
1878
died Jerusalem
Israel
1965

A TRUE PHILOSOPHER: too absorbed in contemplating the meaning of life to indulge in the worldly vanity of shaving. He has been called a 'religious existentialist', a 'mystical pacifist', a 'utopian Zionist' and a 'man who disliked being labelled'. He grew up with his grandparents in Galicia, speaking Yiddish, German, Hebrew, French and Polish, and became a student at Vienna, Zürich and Berlin universities. His writings ranged across fiction, folklore, theology and mysticism, and in the face of modern-day alienation, his philosophy was one of redemption and interconnection. Discovery of Hassidic tradition helped awaken his Jewish faith, and his idea of Zionism was a quest for spiritual, more than political, security.

His most influential work, **I and Thou** (1923), expounded a philosophy of relationship, arguing that the 'I' is developed only through high-quality interaction with others. Man, he says, perceives the world as ordered, detached and reliable. You 'take it to yourself as the "truth", and it lets itself be taken; but it does not give itself to you'. You may also apply that basis to relations with other people (an 'I—It' interaction), but you may also relate in an 'I—Thou' mode in which there is mutual affirmation and opening up. This mode, he warned, is ellusive: any attempt to achieve it or describe it will turn it back into an 'I—It' interaction because it becomes objectified. God, the 'eternal Thou' is a third participant of each 'I—Thou' moment. So, true relations with God are 'I—Thou' experiences, but trying to prove God's existence brings you back into 'I—It' mode. For the Jews, the writing of the *Torah* was a monumental 'I—Thou' interaction between Man and God. Buber suggested that it is also possible to have an 'I—Thou' relationship with the world and the objects in it, through the medium of art, music or poetry.

To the Nazis, all that mattered was that Buber was a Jew. They were not going to have more than a 'we—it' relationship with a man whose writings included **The Tales of Rabbi Nachman** and **On Judaism**, and who edited a monthly journal entitled *Der Jude.* A Nazi review of his Bible translation (a joint effort with Rosenzweig) pilloried it as proof of 'what happens to the German language if it is subjected to Hebrew law and characterised by Hebrew rhythm'.

In 1938 he fled Germany for Jerusalem, where he became a professor of social philosophy. After the war he worked hard to re-establish dialogue between Jews and Germans and also to improve understanding between Israelis and Arabs ... jobs that no doubt required grappling with a lot of 'us—them' moments.

"The world is not comprehensible, but it is embraceable: through the embracing of one of its beings"

13

ERNST BLOCH

born
Geneva
Switzerland
1885
died Portland
USA
1977

UTOPIAN-MARXIST PHILOSOPHER, a pacifist who sat out World War I in Switzerland, then joined the KPD (German Communist Party) during the 1920s. He lived mainly in Berlin until, having spoken out against Nazi politics in press articles, and being on Hitler's list as both bolshevist and half-Jewish, he retreated to Switzerland once again in 1933. Eventually, via Austria, France and Czechoslovakia, he reached the USA where, making little attempt to learn English, he busied himself with German exile politics, alongside Brecht, Feuchtwanger and Heinrich Mann. Sitting in New York Public Library, he completed most of his sprawling, epic philosophical trilogy **The Principle of Hope**. His starting point was the everyday life of the individual, in which he identified a constant stream of wishes, hopes and dreams of a better life, made manifest in stories, travel, advertising, jokes and other kinds of cultural products. Fashion, he saw as offering the potential for transforming ourselves in the eyes of others. Advertising conjures up magical properties in commodities. Phony though these might prove to be, the ubiquity of advertising 'shows the depth of the needs that capitalism exploits and the wishes for another life that permeate capitalist societies'. Wishes and their fulfilment are the bases of fairy tales, and adventure stories portray ordinary people defeating oppression. All these things Bloch saw as 'immature, but honest substitutes for revolution'. He pointed out that Fascism had built a strong base by addressing the simple needs for security, home and community. He considered that the past contained unrealised hopes that could yet be fulfilled, and urged a philosophy of 'dreaming forward'. In fact, the potentials always seemed to him to lead towards socialism: for him, culture had always contained 'red arrows' of possibility, moments of struggle against oppression which pointed towards the socialist utopia.

In 1948 he returned to Germany to lecture in the German Democratic Republic (East Germany). A major conflict erupted between him and the East German Communist Party: Bloch had increasingly criticised them for being inhumane, bureaucratic and failing to practise true socialism. They in turn called him 'anti-Marxist' and stopped him from publishing and lecturing. Hearing of the building of the Berlin Wall while lecturing in West Germany, he decided not to return to the East.

His writings were taken up by the student movement of the late sixties, but, having nailed his colours to the Marxist mast, his reputation declined once it became clear that red arrows were all falling to earth well short of utopia.

"Mankind and the world carry enough good future; no plan is itself good without this fundamental belief within it"

15

EDITH STEIN

born Breslau
Germany
1891
died Auschwitz
Poland
1942

"What did not lie in my plans, lay in
God's plans**"**

ALIAS SAINT TERESA BENEDICTA of
the Cross; the Jewess who became a Catholic nun,
martyr and saint, after a short interlude of atheism and
a high-level academic career in philosophy. 'In my
dreams,' she confessed, 'I always foresaw a brilliant
future for myself.' One of the first women to be admitted
to university, she studied philosophy under Husserl, the
founder of phenomenology. Her dissertation **On the
Problem of Empathy** tackled the critical phenomenological issue of how we are able to know anything at
all about the inner life of other people.

After her dramatic conversion (upon reading the
autobiography of St Teresa of Avila in a single night in
1921), she became a leading Catholic feminist. She
argued that men and women are defined not by biolog-
ical differences but by differences in their soul. Women,
she said, should celebrate their ability to support and
inspire others, to be a kind of 'cultural and spiritual
mother'. She entered a Carmelite convent, to the dis-
tress of her mother, who was deeply hurt by what she
saw as her betrayal of her people in their time of
persecution. In 1933 she unsuccessfully requested an
audience with Pope Pius XI, intending to impress upon
him the increasing plight of the Jews under the Nazis.
Her convent sent her to Holland, partly for her security,
partly for theirs. But she was no safer there: when the
Nazis invaded, she was sent to Auschwitz and gassed.
Having died because of her Jewish birth, she was
nevertheless made a Catholic saint by Pope John Paul II
in 1989. A martyr to some, an apostate to others.

ERICH FROMM

born Frankfurt
Germany
1900
died Muralto
Switzerland
1980

AN ATHEISTIC MYSTIC from an Orthodox Jewish background, who was an influential member of the Frankfurt Institute for Social Research until he fled Nazi Germany in 1934 for the USA. Once in the Land of the Free, he wrote **Escape From Freedom** (1941), a cautionary book naming freedom as one of life's greatest burdens, since it brings isolation and bewilderment which the individual seeks to avoid by retreating into authoritarianism, conformity or destructiveness. He pointed to the alienation of the individual that the capitalist system provokes, leading people to seek security in extreme social systems like Fascism. He saw family life as setting the 'orientation' of an individual towards either a 'having' or a 'being' mode, the latter being more productive in embracing freedom.

Fromm taught at several universities in the USA and Mexico, and became a celebrity in the 1960s for his psychoanalytical theories and as a peace activist. His interest in the economic and cultural roots of personality led him to an approach that blended Freud and Marx. In 1956 he published **The Art of Loving**, a hippie classic and world best-seller, in which he examined love in its many-splendoured forms and suggested we're all too busy trying to be lovable to concentrate on actually loving.

"Man's main task in life is to give birth to himself, to become what he potentially is. The most important product of his effort is his own personality**"**

17

SIGMUND FREUD

born Freiburg
Moravia
1856
died London
England
1939

THE FATHER FIGURE of psychoanalysis, without whom we might never have realised that men can be irrational. He introduced us to the subconscious and showed us our ids, egos and superegos. Now we can recognise Freudian slips and symbols, know when we're being anal and, most importantly, pay someone to listen when we want to go on about ourselves.

The eldest of eight children and his mother's favourite, he graduated in medicine and set up as a neurologist in 1886, treating nervous diseases. At first he used hypnotic suggestion as part of therapy, but soon replaced it with 'free association' in which a patient came up with a series of words at random. Freud's lesson is that such things are in fact not random, but that a whole network of connections exists in our subconscious minds, and that exploring them can help in healing. In the time-honoured fashion of sages of all cultures, he interpreted dreams, believing them to be disguised fulfilment of unconscious wishes. He subjected himself to extensive analysis, unearthing and confronting his own Oedipus complex.

Freud saw the Nazi phenomenon as libido-attachment on a mass scale: the handing over of a collective superego to a single love-object. The Nazis just saw Freud and psychoanalysis as degenerate. And Marxist, of course, and Jewish. In 1933 his books – such classics as ***The Psychopathology of Everyday Life*** and ***The Interpretation of Dreams*** – were burned as 'Jewish pornography'. That same year, he and Einstein co-wrote the polemic ***Why War?*** with little hope of it being heeded (or answered).

When German troops entered Vienna, he was in his 80s, having hung on against advice in the curious hope that the Catholic Church might prove a bulwark against Nazism. The Gestapo searched his house and took away his daughter Anna for 12 hours of interrogation: child's play perhaps to the girl whose father had been psychoanalysing her regularly for years. On her release, she urgently persuaded the family to leave Vienna at once. Thanks to influential friends and a payment of 31,329 Reichsmarks as 'refugee tax', Freud, his wife, his nurse, Anna and their housekeeper escaped to London. His architect son Ernst and grandsons Lucian and Clement were already there, as were many of his followers. But Freud died of jaw cancer only a year later, having asked his doctor for a fatal dose of morphine. All four of his sisters remained in Austria and died in concentration camps.

"Men are strong only so long as they represent a strong idea. They become powerless when they oppose it"

JOHN.
MINNION

19

2

Undesirable

science

When **Hitler** was invited to become Chancellor in January 1933, it did not look like revolution. It was simply that his years of persistent hectoring, backed by loud public support, had born fruit: he was made leader of a democratically elected, bourgeois, right-wing Government of National Unity that contained only two Nazis besides himself. His views seemed not so dissimilar from those of his coalition partners. True, he was backed by some unruly elements and he might do some short-term damage, but he would be tamed by being brought on-side. And he was too preposterous – surely – to survive beyond the upcoming election…

The revolution that people really feared was from the Communists: and when the Reichstag (parliament building in Berlin) mysteriously went up in flames, few doubted Hitler's cry that this was a starting-signal for the Communist uprising, nor resisted the immediate and drastic action that he took. Around 4000 people were summarily rounded up and imprisoned: mainly Communists, but also others – Hitler already had his list. An emergency decree was proclaimed, giving the government power to take extreme measures, including far-reaching constitutional and liberty-curbing changes. Firm leadership, it seemed, had averted the Communist putsch. Then, in March, following the dissolution of the Reichstag, the last 'free' elections were held. Despite intense Nazi intimidation, with daily atrocities, despite the denial to any leftist party of the opportunity to campaign, despite the visible capitulation of the leadership of all the other parties, the people still gave the Nazis less than 44% of the vote. Nevertheless, this was enough for a majority in the new Reichstag. Indeed, the Nazis made sure that an atmosphere of triumph, complete with mass parades, marching bands, flags and fireworks, had washed across the nation and submerged it before polling day had even dawned. Immediately on taking command, Hitler set about introducing the Enabling Law which was to underpin his dictatorship and ultimately ensure Nazi domination over every area of German life.

'Cleansing' began at once. With the gaols quickly filled, a concentration camp opened at Dachau with an initial intake of 200 Communists. A sterilisation programme was started for citizens with congenital disabilities. Virtually all political opponents and Jews in state institutions, including universities, were sacked.

The purge of Jewish scientists was to be one of the gravest of Hitler's self-inflicted wounds. Before 1932, German scientists had been highly successful, winning one-third of all Nobel Prizes for Science; German was widely regarded as the language of science. Over the next 27 years, Britons were to win 21 science prizes, Germans just eight. By the end of the 1930s, 30% of Germany's

timeline

1933

Jan •Hitler becomes Chancellor

Feb •Reichstag fire leads to state of emergency

Mar •Reichstag elections: Nazis win 43.9% of vote, scraping a majority
•Enabling Law passed
•First concentration camp opens at Dachau

Apr •One-day boycott of Jewish shops in Berlin
•Political opponents and Jews in government employment are sacked, including scientists, teachers and civil servants
•Gestapo (Secret State Police) formed

May •Book-burnings
•Trade unions are dissolved

July •Germany is declared a one-party state

Sept •Goebbels establishes Reich Chamber of Culture, barring Jews from participation in the arts

Oct •Jewish journalists are banned from newspapers
•Germany quits League of Nations

Nov •Nazis win 95% in plebiscite endorsing Hitler's foreign policy

21

scientists had left the country and most of them were committing their talents to Germany's enemies. Yet Hitler had no regrets: 'if the dismissal of Jewish scientists means the annihilation of contemporary German science, then we shall do without science for a few years'. He approved of 'authentic', experimental science (Dr Mengele's later work on prisoners at Auschwitz comes to mind), but anything too abstract or theoretical was automatically damned as 'Jewish'. Atomic science he called 'a spawn of Jewish pseudo-science'.

No doubt Hitler would have found an 'authentic' use for an atom bomb if his team of scientists had managed to develop one. Shorn of their best brains and led by Werner Heisenberg – a man whose commitment to the cause was, perhaps deliberately, ambiguous – it proved impossible for them in wartime conditions.

The arrival of first Nazism and then war magnified moral dilemmas for scientists, and their responses varied according to personal vision and temperament. There were inner conflicts between patriotism and loyalty to the international scientific community; more mundane questions of funding and keeping jobs; and private concerns about reputation and posterity. There was also the issue of restraint, especially as the awesome possibilities of nuclear technology became reality. Ironically, it was the pacifist visionaries – Szilard and Einstein – who set the atomic ball rolling for the Allies. The fear of a nuclearised Hitler united scientists of all persuasions behind the Manhattan Project as a deterrent. Yet, when it became clear, in 1944, that Hitler's bomb was a non-starter, only one scientist, Joseph Rotblat, resigned from the Project. 'Scientists must always remember that they are human beings first, scientists second,' he said.

FRITZ HABER

FEW SCIENTISTS HAVE had such a profound effect on the world as this deeply patriotic German, a Protestant convert whose Jewish blood ultimately rendered him 'undesirable' in his beloved homeland.

By the end of the 20th century, the human population had grown to six billion, a number untenable without Haber's breakthrough in the fixing of nitrogen from the air in the form of ammonia, which made possible the artificial fertilisers that have radically increased the growth of crops worldwide. His research started as a response to the British naval blockade that cut off supplies of nitrates to Germany during World War I; and a useful side-product of the process he developed was explosives.

Haber then trumped that by inventing chemical warfare. The first 5000 steel cylinders of chlorine gas were released, at his instigation and under his supervision, near Ypres in 1915, successfully killing and injuring thousands of Allied soldiers in their trenches. His wife, Clara, committed suicide with his army pistol a few days later. A chemistry PhD herself, she was an outspoken anti-militarist, and regarded his endeavours

born Breslau
Germany
1868
died Basel
Switzerland
1934

as 'a perversion of science'. His efforts only prolonged the war without bringing victory, and as Germany faced a heavy reparations bill, Haber set off in a boat on an unsuccessful quest to extract gold from seawater. He was awarded a Nobel Prize for his nitrogen-fixing work, but for violating the Hague Convention that outlawed the use of poisonous weapons, he was named a war criminal and forbidden to work on poison gas. He carried on regardless, and his experiments led directly to the preparation of Zyklon B, which the Nazis later used in the gas chambers. He died too soon 'to see his fellow Germans use this form of killing on his fellow Jews', as his widowed second wife put it, but not too soon to find his patriotism betrayed. He was forced to resign from his post in 1933, having refused to dismiss his Jewish staff. He fled to Cambridge where he had secured a post, but was frostily received and died a disillusioned man.

Haber's work highlights the dilemmas of scientific intention and effect. Acting in the ostensibly noble cause of patriotism, he has left the world a devilish legacy. He developed chemical warfare for the same reason the US built the atom bomb: to have it before the enemy. It prolonged the war and crossed an agreed boundary of human action. With nitrogen fixation he has helped to feed the world, but, at the same time, has left it overpopulated, polluted and dependent on agribusiness.

"In no future war will the military be able to ignore poison gas. It is a higher form of killing"

23

HANS KREBS

born Hildesheim
Germany
1900
died Oxford
England
1981

ENERGY
CONSERVATION
AREA

CATABOLIC
PATHWAY

ANABOLIC
PATHWAY

GLYCO LYSIS

PYRUVATE → CITRAT → CIS-ACONITATE → ISOCITRATE → OXALOSUCCINATE → α-KETOGLUTARATE → SUCCINYL-CoA → SUCCINATE → FUMARATE → MALATE → OXALOACETATE

CoA

CELLS MUST PRODUCE ENERGY to survive. Fortunately our cells have little **Krebs Cycles** wheeling away inside them all the time, like power plants, taking half-digested food as fuel and churning out energy along with water and carbon dioxide. Each revolution of the cycle starts and ends with citric acid, enzymes move back and forth like well-oiled pistons, triggering a hydration here, an oxidation there, and we can get on with life knowing all these things are in hand.

Hans Krebs, who discovered the cogs and cams of this process and got a Nobel Prize for it in 1953, was originally following his surgeon father's footsteps in medicine, but became increasingly interested in the link between physical chemistry and the biology of human metabolism. In December 1932 he was recommended for a lectureship by the dean at Freiburg University, yet within months the very same man signed a letter informing him of his dismissal under the new anti-Jewish laws. He fled to Cambridge, settling happily into British academic life. Soon he was Professor Krebs, then Sir Hans Krebs. In 1965, he presented a £90,000 cheque to the British Academy from the Jewish refugees who had become successful in Britain, and gave a moving speech in which he thanked the British people for welcoming them and giving them a safe new home. Meanwhile, in Germany, his family had survived the war thanks to protection given by a Nazi officer who had had treatment from Krebs Senior.

"I arrived in England with nothing but a sigh of relief"

OTTO MEYERHOF

born Hanover
Germany
1884
died Philadelphia
USA
1951

"All representatives of science… [should] pour the smoothing oil of true wisdom and reasoned self-reflection on the agitated waves of the peoples' national passion**"**

A SINGLE FROG MUSCLE was enough to win a shared Nobel Prize for this biochemist in 1922, when he mapped the fixed relationship between the consumption of oxygen and the metabolism of lactic acid in muscle cells. He was a widely cultured man, drawn not only to medicine, but also to psychology, philosophy and the arts. Hostility to both his Jewishness and his pacifism almost induced him to leave Germany after World War I, but by the time World War II loomed and he had to get out, he was extremely loath to go. At the Kaiser Wilhelm Institute in Berlin his team were near to clarifying the significance of ATP; finding the same quality of assistants and equipment elsewhere in wartime would be impossible. But once it was clear his Nobel status would no longer shield him from the Jewish fate, he and his family left for Paris in a hurry in 1938, abandoning his scientific data and personal belongings. Later, one of his students bought back some of these items in an auction of 'Jewish possessions' and had them sent to him in the USA. Getting to America as the Germans invaded France was a chaotic and hazardous business. Refused the vital French exit visa, the Meyerhofs had to cross clandestinely on foot into Spain, with help from a benevolent diplomat, Hiram Bingham. Another humanitarian, the Emergency Rescue Committee's Varian Fry, helped their son Walter who had become separated from them. Walter (also a scientist) later set up the Varian Fry Foundation in gratitude to the American volunteer who, having arrived with a list of 200, ultimately helped around 1500 exiles to escape from France.

MAX BORN

born Breslau
Germany
1882
died Göttingen
Germany
1970

THE MAN WHO FIRST USED the term 'quantum mechanics' and who developed the **Born Approximation Theory** and the **Born-Haber Cycle**, was also known as 'the founder and undisputed master of lattice dynamics' and has on his gravestone the equation $pq - qp = h/2\pi$. Einstein's famous protestation that 'God does not play dice' stems from a letter to Born, and both men have a moon crater named after them. He was a good pianist, sometimes making music with Heisenberg (also on piano), and sometimes with Einstein (violin).

Born's early interests were maths and astronomy, though his mature achievements were in physics, leading to a shared Nobel Prize in 1954 for work on the movement of subatomic particles. Besides giving it its name, his key contribution to quantum mechanics was to apply a statistical interpretation to wave function.

To the Nazis it was all Jewish and bogus, and they dismissed him – quite courteously – from his directorship at Göttingen. Few scientific institutes suffered as catastrophically from the 'cleansing' of its Jews as did Göttingen, formerly one of the world's great centres of mathematical physics. Though his teaching style was considered formal, even aloof, he was revered by his students, who included Oppenheimer and Heisenberg. Born left Germany for Britain, where from 1936 until his retirement he held the chair of natural philosophy at Edinburgh University. In 1957 he and 17 other nuclear scientists signed the *Göttingen Declaration,* warning of the dangers of holding atomic weapons.

"The belief that there is only one truth and that oneself is in possession of it seems to me the deepest root of all evil that is in the world**"**

26

NIELS BOHR

born Copenhagen
Denmark
1885
died
Copenhagen
Denmark
1962

"An expert is someone who has made every possible mistake in a very narrow field**"**

REVERED GURU OF COPENHAGEN, where he was both founder and lifelong director of the Institute of Theoretical Physics. Bohr studied under Rutherford in Manchester, working on the 'quantum leaps' of electrons that jumped orbits and emitted photons. He received a Nobel Prize in 1922. Strongly committed to the scientific community, he contributed significant insights to the work of fellow physicists. He shared thought experiments with Einstein that persuaded him to be less uncertain of the certainty of uncertainty in quantum theory. His model of the nucleus as a 'water droplet' that could split into two, helped Meitner and Frisch identify uranium fission.

Bohr was an avuncular eccentric with strange speech mannerisms, a fine soccer player (though not as good as his brother, who played for Denmark), and a man who wrestled with the moralities of science. His relationship with his pupil Heisenberg – the brains behind the Uncertainty Principle, and the man who ran Hitler's nuclear programme and may or may not have stymied it – is explored in Michael Frayn's fascinating play *Copenhagen*. It seems Bohr agonised in later years over whether he had given unwarranted impetus to the Manhattan Project: a wartime meeting with Heisenberg had led him to suppose, mistakenly, that a German atom bomb was imminent.

Following the Nazi occupation of Denmark, Bohr, who was partly Jewish, escaped in a fishing boat to Sweden. He ended up on the Manhattan Project. After Hiroshima, he put much effort into working for peace.

ALBERT EINSTEIN

born Ulm
Germany
1879
died Princeton
USA
1955

THE 20TH-CENTURY'S PROMETHEUS who wanted 'to know God's thoughts; the rest are details'. He also felt God was 'subtle, but not malicious', and that He did not play dice, for which reason Einstein could not accept the uncertainties essential to quantum theory. Always contrary, he renounced both his Jewishness and his German nationality in his student years. Later he embraced Zionism, but continued to resist a national identity, calling nationalism 'the measles of mankind'. He once said, 'If my theory of relativity is proven successful, Germany will claim me as a German and France will declare that I am a citizen of the world. Should my theory prove untrue, France will say I am a German and Germany will declare that I am a Jew.' Although he was not a religious Jew, he did much for Jewish causes, and was offered the presidency of Israel in 1952. One reason he turned it down was the fear of 'the development of a narrow nationalism'.

He settled from 1901 in Switzerland, where varicose veins and flat feet helped him to avoid national service.

After failing the entrance exam for Zürich Technical College, he worked in the patent office in Bern, investigating physics in his spare time. He eventually obtained a doctorate in 1905 and then published his **Special** and **General Theories of Relativity**, showing that strange things happen to mass and time as the speed of light is approached. He predicted that light would bend in response to gravity, and when, during a 1919 eclipse, the light from a star was tracked and found to bend as it neared the sun, he became a star himself, ranking with Galileo and Newton as a revisor of conceptual physics. He sometimes put his success down to having been such a slow developer that, as an adult, he was still wondering in childlike ways. 'The only reason for Time,' he liked to say, 'is so that everything doesn't happen at once.'

He received the Nobel Prize in 1921, but already his lectures in Berlin were being disrupted by anti-Semites. Pre-empting exclusion by the Nazis, he gave up his post on the day they came to power and emigrated to the USA to teach at Princeton University. Nazi storm troopers ransacked his house and confiscated his boat. (Sailing was his relaxation, along with playing the violin.) In 1939, he and Szilard wrote a letter to persuade President Roosevelt to start work on making a nuclear bomb before Hitler did. Thus, ironically, this lifelong pacifist goes down in history as one of the fathers of the Bomb.

In 1955 he went to meet his Maker, and is doubtless playing dice with him now.

"Imagination is more important than knowledge. Knowledge is limited. Imagination encircles the world"

$E = mc^2$

JOHN MINNION.

29

LEO SZILARD

born Budapest

Hungary

1898

died La Jolla, California

USA

1964

WAITING BY THE TRAFFIC LIGHTS

near the British Museum in 1933, Leo Szilard suddenly thought up the nuclear chain reaction. If an atom is split by one fired neutron and the process releases two neutrons, these two could be prompted to split two new atoms. And so on, rapidly through billions of atoms, unlocking the energy for a vast explosion. This idea gave the green light for production of an atomic bomb.

Perfectly aware that Hitler would build and use a nuclear bomb if he could, Szilard resisted the scientist's natural impulse to publish, and wrote to fellow scientists who were on the same track, urging discretion. Alas, a more human chain reaction was already in process: a French scientist couldn't resist publishing; a German scientist read the article, sniffed a funding opportunity and approached the War Office. They set up a nuclear research programme; so did the Allies. Then Hiroshima; Nagasaki; nuclear arms race; proliferation; Armageddon… Some chain reactions are uncontrollable.

In December 1942, a successful chain reaction was achieved by Szilard and others in a Chicago squash court. 'This day will go down as a black day in the history of mankind,' he wrote.

Szilard was a physicist and inventor of great vision and insight, known for spending hours in the bath-tub, thinking. If, for instance, he had noticed that day that Berlin women were constantly hitching up their stockings, he would think of a way to hold them up by working iron threads into the stocking tops and sewing magnets into coat pockets. Later in life, he cured himself of cancer by radiation therapy of his own design. He was a Jew who had originally left his native Hungary to avoid anti-Semitism, and he was politically aware enough to see the rising dangers in Berlin. Unlike his older colleague Lise Meitner, who almost left it too late, he realised on the day after the Reichstag fire that it was time to go. Stuffing his life-savings in his shoes he took the train to Vienna, then left for England and eventually the USA.

Szilard was co-signatory of Einstein's letter to Roosevelt. (The two physicists were old friends: they had once attempted to develop an Einstein-Szilard fridge.) He also petitioned President Truman just before the Hiroshima bomb was unleashed, warning that the US 'may have to bear the responsibility of opening the door to an era of devastation on an unimaginable scale'. After the war, having helped the nuclear genie out of the bottle, Szilard was tirelessly involved in political and diplomatic damage-limitation work to prevent the dangers he had always foreseen and feared.

"We turned the switch, saw the flashes, watched for ten minutes, then switched everything off and went home.
That night I knew the world was headed for sorrow**"**

30

31

EDWARD TELLER

born Budapest

Hungary

1908

died Stanford

USA

2003

THE ORIGINAL DR STRANGELOVE, the father of the hydrogen bomb (so much more powerful than a mere atom bomb). Losing his foot under a streetcar in Munich did little to cripple his performance as a mathematical genius, inventive physicist, pianist and ping-pong player. He was a pupil of Heisenberg, and left Germany hastily in 1934 to study with Bohr in Denmark, before emigrating to the USA.

He was central to America's nuclear programme — from the moment he drove Szilard to Einstein's Long Island retreat and witnessed the signing of the fateful letter to Roosevelt. A fellow Hungarian Jew, he held opposing views to Szilard on the moral dimension of science. Indeed, he believed a scientist's job was to inform, leaving morality to the politicians. He saw 'suppression of knowledge' as a crime, and Communism as something even worse.

Throughout the post-war era, he remained totally committed to the US governmental and military view of the deterrent effect of a massive nuclear arms build-up. He worked on the Manhattan Project, and after his faintly damning testimony in the anti-Communist witch hunt against the Project leader, J. Robert Oppenheimer, he lost most of his scientific friends for life. When he proposed increased nuclear testing during the Vietnam War, protesters labelled him a war criminal. In the 1980s he was one of the main advocates of Reagan's Star Wars (SDI) initiative. When his long life ended, one Nobel Prize-winning fellow scientist called him 'an enemy of humanity'.

"We had a wonderful record on the hydrogen bomb. We tested it, perfected it and never used it — and that served to win the Cold War"

LISE MEITNER

born Vienna
Austria
1878
died Cambridge
England
1968

HAVING THE ELEMENT 'Meitnerium' named after her was a posthumous consolation prize for Germany's first female professor of physics. She endured discrimination all the way from her schooling (Viennese high schools only took girls from 1899) to the oversight that caused her to miss out on her share of the Nobel Prize awarded to her colleague, the chemist Otto Hahn. They were the co-discoverers of nuclear fission, working together in Berlin until she fled the Nazis for Sweden. So immersed was she in her work that she almost left it too late to escape; neither her status as a converted Christian nor the protection of her colleagues, Planck and Hahn, could have saved her from the fate prescribed for all Jews. The research continued by correspondence. When Hahn wrote that bombarding a uranium nucleus with neutrons had produced barium, she was able to prove that the nucleus was actually splitting like a separating water droplet.

Perhaps her scientific exile in Sweden, or simply the incoherence of wartime conditions, caused the Nobel committee to underappreciate her role. Maybe there was sexism and anti-Semitism. Doubtless Hahn enjoyed having the limelight to himself, knowing she cared little for it. When in 1945 she heard of the horrors of the concentration camps, she wrote to Hahn 'out of honourable friendship', condemning those scientists (Hahn included) who worked for Hitler 'offering only passive resistance', and cursing herself for not leaving Germany earlier: 'since in effect by staying there I supported Hitlerism'.

"I am not important: Why is everybody making such a fuss over me?"

3

Undesirable

writing

On the night of 10th May 1933, members of the German Student Association displayed their fervour for the Nazi cultural agenda by burning books in university cities. Reich Propaganda Minister Goebbels arrived at midnight at Berlin's Openplatz, outside the Opera House, to address jeering crowds while the flames rose from a pile of 20,000 books by international authors that Hitler had already blacklisted as degenerate or politically unreliable. Names on this list included Helen Keller, damned for being deaf and blind as well as for her socialism; Jack London, who wrote *Call of the Wild*; and Felix Salten, author of the degenerate *Bambi*. As the bonfire blazed, Goebbels proclaimed the 'end of an era of Jewish hyperintellectualism': the future German man would not be 'a man of books, but a man of character'. Student leaders intoned the names and offences of the discredited authors: 'Against debasing exaggeration of man's animal nature, we consign to the flames Sigmund Freud! Against class struggle and materialism: Karl Marx! Against decadence and moral decay: Heinrich Mann!' Other charges included 'condescending debasement of the German language' and 'Jewish-democratic-influenced journalism alien to our people'. Little distinction was made between overtly political writers and those who merely chose themes and modes of expression that were not deemed symbolic of the German spirit. Into the fire went the complete library (over 10,000 books) of Magnus Hirschfeld, the homosexual director of the nearby Institute for Sexology.

Jewish authors were in a minority on this list. Nazi anti-Semitism had been somewhat checked in the early days of 1933 while Hitler astutely targeted his political enemies, particularly the Communists. However, on 1st April, a 'day of national boycott' of Jewish businesses signalled that the spotlight was back on the Jews and going to remain there. Goebbels was probably the most anti-Semitic of Hitler's henchmen and he did his job with flair and zeal. 'He who controls the medium controls the message; he who controls the message controls the masses,' he said. Judging radio to be the key authoritarian medium, he pressed for the mass manufacture of a cheap *Volk* wireless (to be popularly known as the Goebbels Blaster) and had loudspeakers erected in streets and squares. He set up the Reich Chamber of Culture, with sub-chambers for literature, music, film, theatre, journalism and broadcasting. Any practitioner in the arts now had to enrol in the Chamber and could only do so if they were considered racially fit. Thousands began to prepare for exile.

Though all legal opposition parties had now been crushed, Hitler had not achieved enough for the ambitions of Röhm's SA storm troopers. These brown-shirted paramilitary thugs had played a useful role – as bouncers at Nazi events and disrupters at other meetings – in the lead-up to taking power. Now they talked of a 'second revolution', against the bourgeois conservatives. But instead, on the so-called Night of the Long Knives, Röhm and several hundred other SA members (along with other perceived political critics) were rounded up by the SS and summarily shot. Overnight, power passed from the SA to the SS, Hitler's bodyguard. This ruthless bloodletting gave Goebbels an early challenge in presentation. He argued the legality of the suppression, explaining that Hitler's statesmanlike action had saved the people from the nightmare of more general violence. What was unmistakable was that Germany now had a government that would kill its subjects without any pretence of a trial. When the aged President Hindenburg died a few weeks later, Hitler combined the office of chancellor with that of president, and was officially proclaimed Führer. Nobody was inclined to try and stop him.

STEFAN ZWEIG

THERE IS A PHOTOGRAPH of Stefan Zweig lying with his wife on a bed, both dead. Her hand rests on his. Exhausted from their exile and in despair about the relentless march, as it seemed in 1942, towards Nazi victory, they took overdoses of barbiturates together. During those last months in Brazil, with no notes or documents to hand for reference, Zweig wrote **The World of Yesterday**, his poignant memoirs of Viennese life. Born into a well-off family of assimilated Jews, he looked back now on a carefree youth in a city of tolerance, stability and personal freedom; where culture was so much more important than politics, since the old empire no longer had ambitions nor sought military action. Then the archduke was shot in 1914, and everything went up in smoke.

Zweig was an evocative writer with an ability to get inside the psyches of both his fictional characters and the many historical figures — such as Dostoyevsky, Dickens, Nietzsche and Magellan — whose biographies

born Vienna
Austria
1881
died Petropolis
Brazil
1942

"I salute all
my friends!
May it be
granted
them yet
to see the
dawn after
the long
night!
I, all too
impatient,
go on
ahead**"**

he wrote. Much of that insight developed from his close friendship with Freud, as well as from a great deal of travel. He excelled in the short story format, portraying the psychological disarray of unstable, tortured souls, such as the man in **The Royal Game** who briefly becomes world champion after memorising games of chess to cope with solitary confinement in a Nazi gaol.

'Dazed for some days' when, as a young boy, he was patted on the back by Brahms, the adult Zweig found himself head-hunted by the most distinguished composer in 1930s Germany, Richard Strauss, who needed to fill the gap left by the death of his librettist Hofmannsthal. The fact that in Nazi eyes he was thus replacing a half-Jew with a full Jew did not dissuade Strauss from co-opting Zweig in the writing of his opera **The Silent Woman**. Nor did Strauss's accommodation with the Nazis deter Zweig, for whom friendship was a prime gift and always overrode politics. Strauss's loyalty to Zweig, and his determination to keep him involved and credited in the opera, caused its closure after three performances and triggered Strauss's removal from the directorship of the Reich Chamber of Music.

But Zweig was already resigned to exile. His books had been burned and he could see from his Salzburg home the threat gathering beyond the nearby border. He left for London, arriving in time to deliver an elegy at Freud's funeral. He became a British national, but his work, then as now, found little appreciation from an English audience. So he washed up in Brazil, feeling too old to start anew in a culture in which he had no roots. He found the present intolerable and could only look back for pointers to a better future for mankind: 'Even in the abyss of despair in which today, half-blinded, we grope about with distorted and broken souls, I look again and again to those old star patterns that shone over my childhood, and comfort myself with the inherited confidence that this collapse will appear, in days to come, as a mere interval in the eternal rhythm of the onward and onward.'

THOMAS MANN

born Lübeck
Germany
1875
died Zürich
Switzerland
1955

A 19TH-CENTURY PATRICIAN who was led by unfolding events to address through fiction the political, social and cultural upheaval of his time. He did this first as an apolitical onlooker, but gradually as a participant, speaking out against 'these animals' (as he called the Nazis in his diary). He had the intellectual vision to understand the catastrophe that was looming in Germany, and to convey it in literary form with a rich mixture of realism and symbolism.

Like Hitler, Mann revered Wagner: when the Nazis took power, he was away on a European tour delivering a lecture in which he confronted his own disquiet about Wagner's seductive power. For this he was publicly lambasted by pro-Nazi musicians, including Strauss, and decided not to return to Germany. When the Nazis revoked his passport, he was granted Czech citizenship before emigrating in 1938 to the USA, where he taught (like Einstein) at Princeton. He turned at once to aiding the rescue of other artistic exiles from Europe, helping the Emergency Rescue Committee to draw up Varian Fry's initial list of 200. Throughout the war, in monthly BBC radio broadcasts, he addressed German listeners, urging resistance against the Nazis.

His *magnum opus* **Doctor Faustus** was conceived in 1905 as a Faustian tale of an artist who deliberately contracts syphilis, in the hope that before dooming him the disease will heighten his creativity, literally intoxicate him into producing works of genius. By 1943 when, exiled in California, he finally began to write the book, events had mirrored the theme: Nazism, as a disease of the body politic, was delivering Germany both the triumphs and the nemesis in true Faustian style. Mann made his Faustus a modernist composer, and picked the brains of fellow exiles like Krenek, Stravinsky, Adorno and Schoenberg. The latter, seeing his Serialist techniques appropriated by a fictitious character, demanded a written acknowledgement of his intellectual property in the book. The fear of artistic sterility that underlies the story was a preoccupying theme for the self-torturing Mann, recurring in novels such as **Death in Venice**, in which an ageing novelist with writer's block finds creativity restored by infatuation with a beautiful boy. Mann sometimes looked back on his first Nobel Prize-winning success, **Buddenbrooks**, and perceived a naïve creative freedom that he had since become too intellectually hyper-aware to regain.

Mann is generally considered to be Germany's greatest 20th-century author and, after the war, was one of the very few revisiting exiles to be feted in both East and West Germany.

"What we call National Socialism is the poisonous perversion of ideas which have a long history in German intellectual life**"**

1934

Mar •Jewish actors banned from stage and screen

June • Jewish companies can no longer be mentioned on radio

•Night of the Long Knives emasculates Röhm's SA storm troopers

July •Jewish law students prohibited from taking exams

Aug •President Hindenburg dies

•Hitler combines presidency with chancellorship to become Führer

1935

Jan •Germany reclaims Saar region

Sept •Nuremberg Laws enacted: Jews stripped of citizenship, defined as 'not of German blood' and forbidden sexual relations with 'German nationals'

1936

Feb •Gestapo placed above the law

Mar •German army enters the Rhineland

Oct •German pact with Italy

Nov •German pact with Japan

HEINRICH MANN

born Lübeck
Germany
1871
died Santa Monica
USA
1950

"The louder
the deceivers
in their
houses cry
'Freedom!'
the louder
the deceived
on the streets
echo their
cry**"**

MORE LEFT-WING than his younger brother Thomas, and so critical of his politics and lifestyle that he cut all ties with him from 1914 until 1922, when Thomas's views changed. Heinrich is best known for his 1904 novel about bourgeois hypocrisy, **Professor Unrat**, mainly because it was the basis for *The Blue Angel*, the film that made Marlene Dietrich.

When Hitler came to power, he left for France, where he had a following. Then, when France fell, he escaped with his wife and nephew — along with Alma and Franz Werfel — thanks to the Emergency Rescue Committee's Varian Fry, who took them by train from Marseilles to Perpignan. Fry could provide American visas which got people into Spain, but once there, lack of a French exit visa would have them returned to France, and thence to the Nazis. Any applications for these exit visas were forwarded to the Gestapo. Also needed were transit visas, only issued to people who had acquired an onward visa from a Portuguese port. Fry did his best with all this, semi-legally, in a climate of minimal trust or certainty. Despite his 70 years and false papers (name Heinrich Ludwig), Mann and the others managed to cross by foot over the mountain goat trails to the Spanish checkpoint, while Fry took their luggage by train and rejoined them en route to war-torn Barcelona. Mann then took a plane to Lisbon and a ship to the US where, deprived of his European public, he lived out his years poor and unknown. His wife committed suicide. Yet these years also saw some of his best works, including his autobiography, **An Age is Examined**.

FRANZ WERFEL

born Prague

Bohemia

1890

died Los Angeles

USA

1945

ALMA MAHLER'S FINAL HUSBAND, a dumpy, chain-smoking Jewish poet, playwright and novelist, the son of a wealthy Czech glove-maker. He formed a pacifist society with Martin Buber and others, and was accused of treason during World War I. In her book *And the Bridge is Love*, Alma depicts the period of exile that followed their 1940 flight from Austria: a time spent moving back and forth between Paris hotels and a watchtower they rented in Sanary, southern France. When France was invaded, the north was occupied and the south, governed from Vichy, signed an armistice that included an agreement to hand over a list of 'undesirables'. Werfel was high on this list, though his Czech passport saved him from arbitrary arrest as the atmosphere became steadily more anti-Semitic. He had a heart attack in Paris but, clinging to a belief in 'the last shred of Europe', resisted leaving France until almost too late.

The Werfels and their many suitcases zigzagged across Vichy France — Bordeaux, Biarritz, Lourdes, Pau, Marseilles — spending a fortune on taxis, hotels and bribes, bumping into friends all following rumour and hunch in their desperation to get to America. One consul granted them transit visas in return for a book-signing. In Marseilles they found Varian Fry, who shepherded them over the border and on to the ship at Lisbon.

Religious faith was a recurring theme for Werfel: in Lourdes, he had vowed to write a homage to St Bernadette if he ever reached the US, and he did. **The Song of Bernadette** became a successful book and film, helping him to settle in exile.

"The primacy of politics destroys the spirit. It enslaves what ought to dominate"

LION FEUCHTWANGER

born Munich

Germany

1884

died Los Angeles

USA

1958

THE INTERNATIONAL RING of Jewish financiers was trying to destroy the German people as a tubercle bacillus tries to destroy a healthy lung, according to the leader of 'The True Germans', a hysterical character with a 'faint dark moustache', in Feuchtwanger's 1930 novel, **Success**. For some reason this story irritated Hitler, who already had its Jewish author high on his hit list. Feuchtwanger had become a literary star in Britain and the USA after publishing his epic historical novel **Jew Süss**, about Süss-Oppenheimer, the Jewish financial counsellor to the 18th-century Duke of Württemberg. In 1940 the Nazis got their revenge by rehashing this story as an anti-Semitic movie, portraying Oppenheimer as a sly exploiter of hardworking Germans and rapist of the pure Aryan heroine.

Out of Germany when the Nazis came to power, Feuchtwanger stayed out, and the Nazis made do with ransacking his home and library. Like the Werfels, he settled in Sanary, France, where he wrote the first anti-Nazi novel by a German exile. **The Oppermanns** (1933) laid bare to the world the traumas suffered by a Jewish family in contemporary Berlin. Within a year it was translated into ten other languages. He was a brave, sometimes reckless man, a prolific writer intent on making historical novels the vehicle for understanding the present. In France he completed his **Josephus Trilogy** about Flavius Josephus, the Jewish historian living in Rome in the 1st century AD. On the outbreak of war he was interned by the French as an alien, despite his outspoken anti-Nazi views. He was released, then interned again near Nîmes after the invasion of France. His wife Marta aided his escape by enlisting support from the sympathetic American consulate officials Hiram Bingham and Miles Standish. Standish drove to the river where the internees bathed, and bundled Feuchtwanger into the back seat of the car, where he found women's clothes and dark glasses to disguise him as Standish's mother-in-law as they passed through the police roadblocks. Bingham, Varian Fry and others engineered the couple's escape over the Pyrenees to Barcelona, then to Lisbon for the boat to the USA. At one stage Lion disguised his purpose with a Red Cross briefcase, at another point Marta proffered cigarettes to distract the Spanish passport controllers from the all-too-famous name of Feuchtwanger.

In Germany, interest in his work has greatly increased in recent years; but he was always held in suspicion in his adopted USA. He was suspected of Communist sympathies and never granted citizenship.

"Exile made us small and dejected. Yet … it also hardened us and made us great**"**

42

43

ARTHUR KOESTLER

born Budapest
Hungary
1905
died London
England
1983

A TRUE 'WANDERING JEW', Hungarian by birth but psychologically rootless, who lived a restless, driven life and conveyed the unique excitement of it all in fresh, cultured English. He went everywhere and embraced everything, including a number of women who didn't actually want to be embraced. Indeed, revelations of his predatory sexual behaviour, along with drunken car crashes, have tarnished much of his reputation in more recent years.

From Budapest, where his industrialist father financed unlikely inventions (some, like radioactive soap, more dubious than others), he went to study science in Vienna. He discovered Zionism and dropped out to go to Palestine where he was first a farm labourer then a newspaper correspondent. In Berlin in 1930, he became a Communist ('an honourable error', he said later). Journalism and Comintern activities took him via Paris to Russia and Soviet Central Asia; over the North Pole (in a Zeppelin), then to Spain (to cover the Civil War) where he was imprisoned by Franco's forces and marked for execution. Rescued by British diplomacy, he wrote up the ordeal in *Spanish Testament*. He suffered further imprisonment in Vichy France and London's Pentonville gaol, but it all made good grist for the mill of his writing. Betweentimes he joined the French Foreign Legion, then the British army, worked for the Ministry of Information and the BBC. By the 1940s he had written some of his best books, mainly reflecting his life experiences. Most telling was *Darkness at Noon*, a grim political fiction laying bare the Bolshevik mindset and the realities of Stalin's show trials.

As an ex-Zionist (as well as an ex-Communist), he wrote *The Thirteenth Tribe*, arguing that East European Jews were actually Caucasian Khazars and not Chosen People after all. Then he set off to India and Japan in a quest for Eastern mysticism. With *The Ghost in the Machine*, about evolution and the brain, he gave The Police an album title. He set up a Koestler Award of cash prizes for creative achievements by prison inmates and bequeathed money for the foundation of a university chair in paranormal psychology. Having campaigned for voluntary euthanasia, he took his own life when terminal illness set in. His wife and dog went with him. The wife was 22 years younger than him, and healthy. It seems she couldn't face life without him. The dog too, presumably.

"The evils of mankind are caused, not by the primary aggressiveness of individuals, but by their self-transcending identification with groups whose common denominator is low intelligence and high emotionality"

45

KURT TUCHOLSKY

born Berlin
Germany
1890
died Gothenburg
Sweden
1935

"The cruelty of most people
is lack of imagination,
their brutality is ignorance**"**

PETER PANTER, THEOBALD TIGER, Ignaz Wrobel and Kaspar Hauser wrote, between them, a great deal of poetry, polemic, criticism and satire. Actually, they were all pseudonyms for the much-loved and much-hated Berliner, Kurt Tucholsky. 'Against impudence and audacity,' cried the students, as his books were burned. An anti-Semitic website calls him 'Exhibit A' in the explanation of 'why the Jews in Germany were hated'. Like most satirists he mocked the establishment from a leftist position, irritating the bumbling Weimar politicians and infuriating the Nazis. He co-edited the theatre magazine *The World Stage*, turning it into a forum for left-wing intellectuals. Like Eisler, Heartfield, Grosz and Brecht, Tucholsky was part of the satirical cutting edge in 1920s Berlin, a time when artists thought they might perhaps change society. He combined his text with John Heartfield's montages in **Deutschland, Deutschland Über Alles** (1929), an attack on philistinism and brutality in Weimar Germany. It sold 48,000 copies in a year and made him many enemies.

He got out while he still could, divorcing his wife by mutual agreement for her safety. He settled in Sweden, near **Castle Gripsholm**, which became the title of his novel — an unexpectedly idyllic, unpolitical story of four young people on holiday. His poems, some satirical, some lyrical, were collected by radical singer/actor Ernst Busch and performed to music by Hanns Eisler. Tucholsky began to have health problems with his sense of smell and taste. In 1935 he committed suicide.

46

ANDRÉ BRETON

THE POPE OF SURREALISM, which was a literary movement at the outset – spawned from the ideas of Freud, whom Breton had met. He studied medicine and psychiatry, and joined the Communist Party – but left in 1935, disgusted with Stalin's autocratic behaviour. Yet he ruled the Surrealists with a ruthlessness Stalin would have been proud of: he was a dogmatic and moralistic demagogue, a control-freak not averse to a purge or two of his own. He remained a Marxist, and was a friend of Trotsky's, but the revolution he demanded was psychological, an emancipation of the subconscious mind. He wrote three verbose Surrealist manifestos and kept the movement pure with regular excommunications. Earlier he had flirted with Dada: 'none of the anti-authoritarianism of Dada rubbed off on him. None of the humour either' remembered Hans Richter, who was unnerved by his 'penetrating, leonine gaze'. Whereas Dadaism was an artistic rebellion of adolescent anarchy, Surrealism was serious, grown-up stuff. He described it as 'pure psychic automatism': free thought unencumbered by reason, aesthetics or morality, and fed by dreams, chance, insanity, the occult and the subconscious. He indulged in 'automatic writing', the poet's version of Freud's 'free association', in books with titles like **Soluble Fish**. The Nazis never really took to it: when they occupied France, Breton fled to the USA.

born Tinchebray
France
1896
died Paris
France
1966

"The mind is ripe for something more than the benign joys it allows itself in general**"**

47

PRIMO LEVI

born Turin
Italy
1919
died Turin
Italy
1987

FEW JEWS SURVIVED AUSCHWITZ. Primo Levi was one, an Italian chemist fortunate to be abandoned in the infirmary with scarlet fever when the Nazis left the camp, driving the 'fit' inmates on a forced death march. He subsequently fulfilled his need and duty to witness in two books, **If This Is A Man** and **The Truce**, which he had some difficulty getting published. These lucid, unflinching, sober, unself-indulgent accounts tell first of the details of day-to-day survival in the camp, and then of the long road home to Italy across war-ravaged Europe.

Auschwitz was a complex of camps, and Monowitz, the one he was assigned to, provided slave labour for the Buna synthetic rubber factory of I.G. Farben. Though not affected when he later revisited the main Auschwitz site, now a museum, Levi felt 'violent anguish' on visiting Birkenau camp, which he had never seen as a prisoner. It has been left virtually unchanged, and its bleak entrance tower and railway track are a graphic memorial seared onto the 20th-century landscape.

Levi became one of Italy's great writers, with books such as **The Periodic Table** and **The Wrench**. He died tragically, falling down the stairwell of the building in which he was born and to which he had returned, against all odds, to live. It looked like suicide, triggered by depression and the ghosts that haunted him. But violent suicide, with no note left, seemed alien to the spirit and style of the man, a negation of his great struggle for survival. He was weak from a recent operation: it may have been an accident.

"Perhaps one cannot, what is more one must not, understand what happened, because to understand is almost to justify**"**

ELIAS CANETTI

born Ruse
Bulgaria
1905
died Zürich
Switzerland
1994

HIS FIRST LANGUAGE was Ladino, the archaic Spanish dialect his Sephardic Jewish ancestors had brought to Bulgaria, where Canetti was born. His second tongue was Bulgarian, his third English, which he began learning when, aged six, he moved with his family to Manchester. Later, in Vienna, he learned German, which became his language of choice as a writer. After completing a PhD in chemistry in 1929, he wrote his first and only novel **Auto-da-Fé** which was largely ignored by everyone except the Nazis, who banned it. After the *Anschluss*, he emigrated to England, eventually settling in Hampstead, London.

His extended essay **Crowds and Power** (1960) grew out of his first-hand experience of the rioting that led to the burning of the Vienna Palace of Justice in 1927, and of the subsequent crowd appeal of Fascism. Canetti saw the crowd instinct as a basic survival mechanism, and considered how and why crowds obey rulers. He defined power as being able to let others die for oneself, and presented Hitler as being as fascinated by his crowds as they were by him. Our task, he suggests, is somehow to control the 'survivor mania' of our rulers by means of 'humanisation of command'.

The charismatic Canetti attracted women. Novelist Iris Murdoch, his lover for three years, based several sexually alluring and controlling mage-like characters on him and dedicated *The Flight from the Enchanter* to him.

He was awarded the Nobel Prize for Literature in 1981 and chose to be buried in a grave next to James Joyce in Zürich.

"The lowest form of survival is killing**"**

49

JOSEPH ROTH

born Brody
Galicia
1894
died Paris
France
1939

"German Jews are doubly unhappy: they not only suffer humiliation, they endure it. The ability to endure it is the greater part of their tragedy"

50

'THE WORLD NEVER ASKS the wanderer where he's going, only ever where he's come from. And what matters to the wanderer is his destination, not his point of departure.' The translations of Michael Hofmann brought Roth's work to English readers, starting with **The Wandering Jews**, collected from the journalism he filed from scattered East European *shtetl* communities in the 1920s, when he was a journalist for the *Frankfurter Zeitung*. Reporting from the edges of Europe and on the dismantling of the Habsburg Empire, his themes were decline and dispossession. He hankered after a fatherland, which made him – for a man who was known as 'Red Roth' (*Der Rote Roth*) when he worked for leftist Viennese newspapers – a bit of a nostalgic conservative. In his most famous book, **The Radetsky March**, he made plain a yearning for the days of the Empire which meant a lot more to him than his Jewish roots, though he understood the Jewish psyche so well. Such feelings of a lost national identity gave him empathy with the homeless, and were reinforced when the Nazis took power. He saw it all coming: he had mentioned Hitler by name as early as 1923, in his first novel **The Spider's Web**, and sensed the great dangers for the Jews: 'the European mind is capitulating', he wrote in 1933. His books were burned; he fled and cut all ties with Germany, settling – in as much as he ever settled – in Paris. Uprooted and dispossessed like those he wrote about, he lived out his last years at – and under – café tables, drinking himself to death and writing six novels and much journalism in the process.

ERIC HOBSBAWM

born Alexandria

Egypt

1917

"Few things are more dangerous than empires pursuing their own interest in the belief that they are doing humanity a favour**"**

THE YEAR OF REVOLUTION saw the birth of both the Soviet Union and Eric Hobsbawm. Hobsbawm's Marxism has outlasted that of the USSR because it is his unassailable faith, born in the heady years of anti-Nazi action in the 1930s, and surviving the revelations of Stalin's crimes and Soviet repression in Hungary (1956), Czechoslovakia (1968), and the East European regime collapses at the end of the 1980s. He joined the Party at 14, having arrived in Berlin from Vienna. There was, he says, 'a feeling the Old World was coming to an end', and it was clear at once on which side he should fight in the battle for a new world. 'We either have socialism or we have barbarism.' He never forgot the thrill of being on the last legal march of the Communists before Hitler came to power and banished such events. With thousands of comrades being rounded up daily, he dodged police to leaflet workers' flats. At 16 he left for England, not in flight (though he qualified for Hitler's list as both a bolshevist and Jew) but, possessing English nationality from his father, to find work and study at Cambridge. He became a respected historian, publishing an accessible four-volume account of world history from 1789. *The Age of Revolution*, *The Age of Capital* and *The Age of Empire* were followed by *The Age of Extremes*. This last book drew on his personal experience — a privilege for any historian — of having been at the right place at the right time.

For a while, until the late nights got the better of him, he was jazz critic for the *New Statesman*.

51

GEORGE WEIDENFELD

born
Vienna
Austria
1919

'DROP THE ARTHUR, DROP THE FELD' said the BBC programme producer to Arthur Georg Weidenfeld, a refugee who had fled Nazi-occupied Austria with a postal order for 16/6d and a three-month visa. 'Surname too long, first name transmits poorly on short wave.' So George Weiden became BBC European correspondent and unleashed his formidable energy into a lifetime of garnering connections. Contacts in the emigré world and within the governments-in-exile informed his broadcasting, and were joined by other names until, several years on, George's network was one of the largest on the planet, and he was Lord Weidenfeld, the hugely successful English entrepreneur publisher. He started Weidenfeld & Nicolson on returning from a sabbatical year in Israel as President Weizmann's Chef de Cabinet. He took on Vita Sackville-West's son, Nigel, as partner and foil: an early controversial best-seller (Nabokov's *Lolita*), and they were away.

British publishing was greatly enriched by Hitler emigrés. The Viennese firm Phaidon, for example, specialised in books of fine art reproductions of a sort rarely seen in Britain. When the Nazis denounced it as a 'vulture publishing house', the Jewish owner, Béla Horowitz, escaped to London, where prescient action had already made Phaidon a technical subsidiary of a British firm. Like Horowitz, refugees Walter and Eva Neurath found English culture so much less visual than verbal, and formed Thames & Hudson, a publishing house dedicated to bringing well-produced books on art to a British readership.

"I yearned to … turn my condition of being with the English but not of the English into an advantage**"**

ANNE FRANK

born Frankfurt
Germany
1929
died Bergen-Belsen
Germany
1945

THE PAPERS ON THE FLOOR, scattered from a briefcase as Gestapo officers arrested the eight Jews and ransacked their hiding-place, were to become an all-time best-selling book, translated into more than 60 languages. For schoolchildren now, Anne Frank's **The Diary of a Young Girl** is likely to be the prime introduction to the enormity of the Holocaust.

During the German occupation of Holland, 24,000 Jews were hidden, often sustained by non-Jewish Dutch at great personal risk. A third were discovered or betrayed, and deported to deathcamps. Otto Frank had moved his family from Germany to Amsterdam in 1933: his four-year-old daughter, Anne, grew up speaking Dutch. Always bright and articulate, she was delighted to receive a diary for her 13th birthday. 'I want to write,' she said, 'but more than that, I want to bring out all kinds of things that lie buried deep in my heart.' And, starting just before their retreat into the hiding-place her father had prepared above his office, she proceeded to record her daily life, alternating the ordinary concerns of a teenage girl and the frustrations of their claustrophobic existence with broader observations: responses to the news of war and persecution as it reached them by rumour and radio. A BBC mention of the importance of war diaries led her to tidy up earlier entries with publication in mind. Anne Frank stands for all the human promise snuffed out by Nazism. Her hopes of becoming a great writer went with her to an early death; yet the words she did have time to write have reached numbers of people that some great writers might envy.

"There is nothing we can do but wait as calmly as we can till the misery comes to an end. Jews and Christians wait, the whole earth waits; and there are many who wait for death**"**

53

4

Undesirable sport

'**I intend to have an athletic youth,**' said Hitler, adding (as if the two were mutually exclusive) 'I will have no intellectual training. Knowledge is ruin to my young men.' From the start, fitness and regimentation were promoted by Hitler Youth groups along with hiking and callisthenics; and when they took power in 1933, the Nazis greatly increased school curriculum time for activities like boxing and cross-country running.

For Goebbels, the sole point of sport was 'to strengthen the character of the German people, imbuing it with the fighting spirit and steadfast camaraderie necessary in the struggle for its existence'. Fundamentally different from this philosophy was the ethos of peace and friendly competition between different nations that characterised the Olympic Games. So when Hitler, on becoming Reich Chancellor, found himself scheduled to host the 1936 Olympics in Berlin, he at first reacted with contemptuous indifference. In the aftermath of World War I, Germany had been excluded from the 1920 and 1924 Olympics; in response, the Nazi newspaper *Der Stürmer* had dismissed the Games as an 'infamous festival organised by Jews'. But the choice of Berlin by the IOC as the 1936 venue signalled the sporting world's commitment to mending bridges.

It was the ever-savvy Dr Goebbels who managed to persuade his Führer of the potential of the Berlin Olympics, both as a source of foreign currency and as a showcase for the 'New Germany'. Once convinced, Hitler committed full support and resources. Now, he decided, it had to be a spectacular triumph.

The Reich Sports Office set up national training schemes to bond athletes together, and designated ethnic guidelines to purge non-Aryans from all levels of sport. The Aryan ideal of firm, lean blonds with rippling muscles was soon to be seen on magazine covers and posters everywhere. Jews, meanwhile, were being excluded from German sport regardless of their prowess. Amateur champion Erich Seelig was expelled from the national boxing association; Daniel Prenn, the nation's's top-ranked tennis player and world number six, was removed from Germany's Davis Cup team. Sports clubs were ordered to set aside October 1935 for teaching anti-Semitism.

Hitler and the Nazis, it seemed, were openly flouting the Olympic code of equality among races and religions; the international reaction, and above all that of the American Olympic Committee (AOC), was going to be vital. There were worldwide calls for a boycott of the whole event. That the Games went ahead with 49 competing countries – more than ever before – and only Ireland boycotting, was a major victory not only for Hitler but for AOC President Avery Brundage. In 1934, Germany set up spurious 'Olympic training courses' for Jewish athletes, and after a brief, carefully supervised visit to Germany, Brundage pronounced himself convinced that German-Jewish athletes were being treated fairly. American athletes, he said, should not get involved in a 'Jew-Nazi fight'. In a close vote, the US Amateur Athletic Union rejected the call for a boycott, and other countries fell into line.

timeline

1931
- Berlin chosen to host 1936 Olympic Games

1932
- Los Angeles Olympics poorly attended because of the Depression

1933
- 'Aryans only' policy imposed on German sports organisations
- American Amateur Athletic Union calls for a boycott of the Berlin Games

1934
- AOC president Avery Brundage visits Germany and is satisfied that Jewish athletes are treated fairly
- AOC votes unanimously to send an American team to Berlin

1935
- Nuremberg Laws come into force

1936
- Germany hosts Winter Olympics at Garmisch-Partenkirchen
- German troops march into the Rhineland
- Berlin Olympics go ahead with 4,066 athletes from 49 countries participating

Opposition, however, was still widespread and vocal. An alternative 'People's Olympiad' was planned in Barcelona, only to be scuppered at the last moment by the outbreak of the Spanish Civil War. Individual athletes announced their personal boycott. For instance, a trio of champion Austrian swimmers, all Jewish, declined to compete; their names were stripped from the records and they were banned for life from all competitions.

Black American athletes responded more ambiguously. To many, racial prejudice in Germany was going to be no worse than that which they suffered at home. This was a chance, they felt, to prove something to their fellow countrymen and the world. Indeed, Black Americans were to capture 14 medals, and Jesse Owens, with four golds, became – and remains – the hero of the Olympics, not least to ordinary Germans, who cheered him on with chants of 'Oh-vens! Oh-vens!'

The opening day arrived. A 900-foot Zeppelin, marked with swastikas, towed an Olympic flag over the crowd of 110,000. Richard Strauss conducted a Wagner march, and the final runner of a relay arrived with a torch first lit from the flame at Olympia, Greece – a Nazi innovation justifiably retained to this day. As 20,000 pigeons were released into the sky, Hitler opened the games with a single sentence. He was silent in public for the rest of the event.

It was a triumph. Overall, Germany won the lion's share of medals; the swastikas outweighed the Olympic heraldry. Participants and spectators alike were treated lavishly. Publicity was inspiring, a colourful fusion of Aryan mythology and Ancient Greek iconography. The Games, said the *New York Times*, brought Germans 'back in the fold of nations'. And *Olympia*, Leni Riefenstahl's film documentary, won first prize at the 1938 Venice Film Festival. But the accolade was skin deep: visitors remained unaware of the rigorous media censorship, and the 600 gypsies who were 'swept from the streets', along with the litter and (for the moment) the anti-Semitic signs.

HELENE MAYER

born Offenbach
Germany
1910
died Munich
Germany
1953

'A CUTE LITTLE MAN' was what Helene Mayer called Hitler, pointing to the picture on her mantelpiece in which the Führer posed, shaking hands with the long-legged blonde fencing champ – Hitler opted out of handshakes at the Olympics in case he was caught clasping the wrong-coloured hand. But this was not the only way Helene was exceptional. Despite her Aryan looks, she was the only Jew in the German team. Her actions, along with those of AOC chief Avery Brundage, were pivotal in staving off the boycott and ensuring a total public relations coup for the Nazis.

She grew up excelling in skiing, horseriding, swimming and ballet. But fencing was her passion and she was just 17 when she won the gold medal in the 1928 Olympics – the first Games after World War I to which Germany was invited. For several years in the run-up to the 1936 Games she lived in Los Angeles – not least because anti-Jewish laws had caused the Offenbach Fencing Club to expel her, despite all the kudos it had gained from her achievements.

Olympic rules forbade athletes to represent more than one country, so Helene was eager to compete for Germany again, regardless of pleas from fellow countrymen such as Thomas Mann (whom she dismissed as a 'meddler') for her to join the boycott. To the Nazis she was a godsend: perhaps the greatest female fencer ever, and every inch (around 70 in height) a patriot. A little temporary redefinition classed her in German eyes as Aryan, since she had less than three Jewish grandparents; whilst international eyes could see her as a Jew given a fair chance to compete. Her citizenship was restored, the normal sporting qualification process was waived, and the press were ordered to resist all mention of her ethnicity.

This time she won silver; on the podium she saluted the Führer, as all German winners did. But when she became world champion the following year, the German press ignored her: it was back to business as usual for anti-Semitism. Returning to the US, she became foil champion eight times, and gave many defiant speeches, lambasting those 'windbags, who still cannot get over the fact that the Olympics in Berlin were the highlight of all the Olympics'. When bone cancer killed her several years after the war, she still had not confronted the true extent and vile nature of the whole Nazi enterprise, and her unwitting part in it. In normal times, hers would have been a resounding success story. But the 'cute little man' made a puppet of her, and she never acknowledged it. She wasn't the first or last to wistfully contend that politics and sport don't mix.

"The Olympic Games are for international sportsmen and women and not for politicians"

GRETEL BERGMANN

born Laupheim
Germany
1914

THE NAZIS PLAYED A CRUEL GAME with Gretel Bergmann. In 1933 her place as a student at Berlin's College of Physical Excercise was put on hold, and the soccer club at Ulm, where she had grown up playing both handball and soccer on equal terms with the men, banned her and all other Jews. She left for England, trained hard, became the 1934 British high jump champion and set her sights on a place in the 1936 British Olympic team. That was when the Nazis started taking an interest. She received an invitation, coupled with veiled threats to her family, to return to the Fatherland, promising the opportunity to train with 20 other Jewish athletes in special courses set up just in time to impress the visiting American Olympic chief Avery Brundage. But while Aryan athletes trained intensively in special camps, these Jews struggled, deprived of cash, coaches and facilities. Even so, Gretel, with one month to go to the Olympics, equalled the German high jump record of 5'3" (1.6m).

Two weeks before the Games, with the American team already committed and protest petering out, Gretel was informed her performance was not good enough to make the team. Stung, she left for the USA, vowing never to return. Her fellow athletes were told she was injured – something she only found out decades later.

Germany therefore entered only two of the allowed three competitors for the women's high jump; they finished in third and fourth places, and the fourth-place jumper later revealed she was a man. But rather a man than a Jewess. The winning jump? 5'3" (1.6m).

"Supposing I win… what do I do? I'm going to stand on that podium and say 'Heil Hitler!'? I mean, this to do for a Jewish girl would never do!**"**

JOHANN 'RUKELIE' TROLLMANN

born Wilsche bei Gifhorn
Germany
1907
died Neuengamme
Germany
1943

"I only want to box, why don't they let me do this any more?**"**

GYPSIES WERE ON HITLER'S LIST, lumped with Jews, Slavs and Negroes as threats to German purity. Trollmann was a Sinto gypsy, talented, charismatic and popular, who had the misfortune to hit the highpoint of his career in the first months of Nazi rule.

In June 1933, when the light-heavyweight title became available because the Jewish holder Erich Seelig had fled the country, Trollmann fought Adolf Witt and ran rings around him. But the judges, on the orders of the Nazi chairman of the Boxing Authority, declared a draw. So incensed were the spectators that the result was hastily reassessed as a win for Trollmann. The new champion wept for happiness. Eight days later he was stripped of his title, 'poor behaviour' (weeping) and 'bad boxing' (?) being cited as reasons.

The Authority now set out to destroy him as a boxer, by demanding that he stand toe to toe with his next opponent and not employ his trademark 'hit-and-move' style (the celebrated 'dance of Trollmann'). Defiantly, he entered the ring as an Aryan caricature – hair dyed blond and flour on his face. He lost. Before long he was reduced to doing turns in circus booths. He divorced his non-Sinto wife for her protection; then, hoping to stave off internment, he agreed to sterilisation. He served briefly on the Eastern front, but was arrested when on leave and dumped in a concentration camp. Now a starving wreck, he was forced to engage in grotesque one-sided bouts with the well-fed guards. Eventually they shot him. Trollmann's brief championship was only acknowledged in the record books in 2003.

5

Undesirable art & design

Hitler knew about art. He was, after all, an artist himself, though his ambitions had been thwarted early on, and he had, unfortunately, never felt able to give up the day job. Sales of *Mein Kampf* had enabled him to buy a collection of works he admired and, in 1937, he opened an exhibition called Great German Art, in Munich – the birthplace of the Nazi Party. He oversaw the selection himself, ensuring that exhibits were all simple to understand and had passed the racial purity test. There were paintings of young people working in the fields; families taking meals or sitting happily together at home; blond Aryan men and women, classically posing in front of Greek temples; and there were portraits of Hitler himself– one as a knight in armour. Soldiers were painted neat and sterile, returning unharmed and unsoiled from the battlefield. In the National Socialist state, the job of the artist constituted a public duty. 'Art,' said Hitler, must be 'the herald of the sublime and beautiful, and thus the bearer of the natural and healthy.' It should also express the eternal values of the *Volk* and

capture the spirit of progress. Opening the exhibition, Hitler spoke for an hour and a half along these lines. There were over 420,000 visitors.

A day later, across the street, there opened a contrasting exhibition of Degenerate Art. This was the centrepiece of the Nazis' programme to rid German art of what Hitler called the 'morbid excrescences of insane and degenerate men'. From the moment of taking power, the Nazis had been replacing museum and gallery staff they considered unsound, and purging their collections of undesirable items. Art criticism was reined in, replaced by 'art reports' that should describe rather than evaluate works of art. The SS raided the homes and studios of banned artists to stamp on any further degeneracy, even checking if paintbrushes were still wet. Painter Willi Baumeister saved his own skin during a raid, by explaining that his abstract paintings were experiments in camouflage technique, for the benefit of the German army.

From the colossal haul of confiscated pieces, a selection was now assembled for the exhibition, which was to be a travelling freak show, ridiculing and condemning its exhibits. It proved to be a blockbuster, with over two million visitors. The exhibits were organised in groups, with plenty of labels to guide visitors in their condemnation. There was 'Marxist propaganda against military service' (eg Grosz and Dix), artists who 'saw the whole world as one huge whorehouse', or whose work was indistinguishable from the daubs of children or the mentally ill. After the exhibition, Goebbels arranged for some of the works to be sold abroad, raising valuable foreign currency, and then burned the rest (5000 works) outside Berlin's main fire station.

In the early decades of the 20th century, Germany and Austria emerged from a period of artistic slumber to be the centre of new movements. The most virile of these was Expressionism: groups like *Die Brücke* and *Der Blaue Reiter*, who distorted form and colour to evoke an inner world of extreme emotion. The outer world was

timeline

1937
July •Great German Art and Degenerate Art exhibitions open in Munich
Sept •Systematic closure or takeover of Jewish businesses begins
Nov •Hitler outlines war plans to military leaders
•The Eternal Jew exhibition opens in Munich, vilifying Jews and attracting 5000 visitors a day

1938
Apr •Jews forced to declare assets
July •Jewish doctors banned from practising medicine on non-Jews
Sept •Jewish lawyers stripped of licences
Oct •Jewish passports marked 'J', thus making unsanctioned emigration virtually impossible
Nov •Jewish children barred from German schools

expressed unsparingly by the social awareness of Käthe Kollwitz and the New Objectivity of Otto Dix and Max Beckmann. The cultural hothouse of Germany's new Weimar Republic also saw the growth of the anti-war, anti-art anarchy of the Dadaists, and the new theories of Freud released the flood of subconscious images that epitomised Surrealism. A great deal of this creative energy and extremity was stirred up by the catastrophe of World War I. The spirit of Modernism that it engendered was to spread across the globe and across the century.

Goebbels, a cultured man, had originally believed Nazism could be 'the carrier of the most progressive modernity'. Expressionism, in particular, he felt, could be viewed as symbolic of the impetus and vigour of the young Nazi movement. But Hitler stepped in. Expressionism, with its colours and distortions influenced by non-European cultures, its affirmation of personal emotion and response to social issues, ran counter to his agenda of 'blood and soil' *Volk*ishness and purity of German values. His rejection had a steely edge: 'It is clear that … there are men who on principle feel meadows to be blue, heavens green, the clouds sulphur-yellow. Either these "artists" do really see things in this way and believe in that which they represent – then one has to ask how the defect in vision arose, and if it is hereditary the Minister of the Interior will have to see to it that so ghastly a defect shall not be allowed to perpetuate itself – or, if they do not believe in the reality of such impressions, but seek on other grounds to impose them upon the nation, then it is a matter for the criminal court.'

By seeing it as a disease carried by 'racial aliens', threatening the healthy soil of the Aryan Germanic nation, Hitler tapped into a widespread fear of Modernism as being not a rich, imaginative flowering, but a symptom of the decline of a civilisation, with echoes of the fall of the Roman Empire. Having applied the herbicide, he now waited – in vain – for the new great German art to bloom.

OSKAR KOKOSCHKA

born Pöchlarn
Austria
1886
died Montreux
Switzerland
1980

EXECUTION WITHOUT TRIAL was what the Gestapo promised him if they ever caught him. 'Kokoschka will be strung up from the nearest lamp post' announced German radio, after the artist had pasted up posters all over Prague about the child victims of the Nazi air attack on Guernica. When a third of his pictures were confiscated and many of them destroyed after the Degenerate Art Exhibition, his ironic response was to paint **Portrait of a Degenerate Artist**. He fled to London in 1938. Lucky to get returned tickets, he and his future wife, Olda, escaped with just hand-luggage, £10 in cash and a self-portrait.

An Austrian student of Gustav Klimt, he was befriended by Adolf Loos, the architect who believed that 'ornament is crime' and who impressed upon the young artist his respect for classical forms. As a painter Kokoschka was a loner — never a card-carrying Expressionist, yet expressionist to the bone, intense and instinctive in his response to experience. Unlike the flat surfaces and colour-charged shapes favoured by the *Brücke* and the *Blaue Reiter* movements, his forms were direct and rough-hewn, with no attempt made to hide the frantic activities of the brush. In early days he would use his bare hands to scrape and smear the paint onto canvas. Flesh looked like raw meat, skies like well-used palettes. He painted broad vistas of the cities his perpetual wanderings took him through; and portraits, always from life, rarely with preliminary sketching: 'I find that neither routine nor technique is of any help.' He was never tempted to follow the path of abstraction. From his passionate affair with Alma Mahler — 11 years his senior — came his famous **Bride of the Wind** (aka *The Tempest*) showing the lovers lying adrift in a dark swirl of stormy waves. He maintained that one night with Alma gave him energy for a week's creative work, and when she left him for Walter Gropius he commissioned a life-size doll in her likeness, using it as a model and occasionally taking it out to restaurants.

He was a brave man, surviving periods of extreme penury, and being left for dead on the Russian front in 1915, with a bullet in his head and a pierced lung. He lived to a ripe old age, always ploughing his own furrow — gouging it out in his determination to get to the soul beneath the surface of life. Besides painting he wrote poetry, plays, essays and stories, often illustrating them. At the end of World War II he paid to have his lithograph **Christ Helps the Hungry Children** displayed at all London Underground stations, in a plea to the Allies to take mercy on the defeated Germans.

"From the stereotype of man as a herd-animal, which lies within every one of us, only decisive experience can release us**"**

ERNST LUDWIG KIRCHNER

born Aschaffenburg

Germany

1880

died Davos

Switzerland

1938

ARTIST AS SELF-DESTRUCTIVE genius. In 1905 he co-founded *Die Brücke* (The Bridge), the first defining movement of Expressionism: a prolific and influential group who held 70 exhibitions in eight years. These artists tried to put clear blue water between themselves and the academic conventions of the past — clear *yellow* water, perhaps, as no self-respecting Expressionist would paint water blue. They probed inward for their inspiration, reflecting emotional states with outrageous colours and distortions of form. Agitated, directional brushstrokes were Kirchner's hallmark, around flat panes of garish colour. His reputation was bolstered by the perceptive admiration of a critic called Louis de Marsalla (actually a pseudonym for Kirchner himself). He painted hectic Berlin city scenes and prostitutes — plus a great number of nudes, sometimes in bunches: he usually kept a few lying around in his studio, ready for the wild, drug-fuelled parties the neighbours always complained of. He also made many prints, which, said de Marsalla, 'mirror the sensations of a man of our time'.

World War I was the undoing of him. He suffered a nervous breakdown and was discharged from the army into a series of sanatoriums, where treatment left him with a morphine addiction. He found respite painting the pink and turquoise scenery of Alpine Switzerland, but never regained good health. After the Nazis damned him as degenerate, and fearful of the spread of their power into Switzerland, he began destroying his own pictures, then shot himself in the heart.

"The work arises as an impulse, in a state of ecstasy, and even when the impression has long taken root in the artist, its recording is nevertheless swift and sudden" *Louis de Marsalla*

EMIL NOLDE

born Nolde
Germany
1867
died Seebüll
Germany
1956

"The artist need not know very much; best of all let him work instinctively and paint as naturally as he breathes or walks**"**

BEING A NAZI was no guarantee against being branded a degenerate and having the rug pulled from under your career. Nolde, a sometime member of *Die Brücke*, was an early convert to Nazism. Born Emil Hansen (he later took the name of his birthplace near the Danish border), he was a religious, nationalistic, outdoor, 'blood and soil' sort of man. Goebbels admired his 'Nordic Expressionism' and decorated his office with his pictures — only to take them down hastily when Hitler disapproved. Nolde was distressed to find his work included in the Degenerate Art Exhibition. In 1941, the Nazis ordered him to cease painting altogether; but he carried on secretly, producing thousands of watercolours which he called his 'unpainted pictures' — intending one day to work them up in oils. In fact, his watercolours were always very powerful, with intense indigos, violets and vermilions spreading and bleeding into each other, saturating the absorbent paper. He was intoxicated by colours — 'it seemed to me as if they loved my hands' — but his forms, especially figures, could be crude. He had the landscape painter's feel for place. Typical is **Tropical Sun**, painted on an extensive trip to the South Pacific, in which reflections of a blistering red sky glow like molten metal in a forest-green sea.

As if it wasn't enough that the Nazis confiscated over a thousand of his pictures from museums, an Allied air raid hit his Berlin studio in 1944, destroying hundreds more. He had kept himself mainly away from the city, in the isolated house and studio he had spent ten years designing and building at Seebüll, north Germany.

GEORGE GROSZ

born Berlin
Germany
1893
died Berlin
Germany
1959

HE HATED THE BOURGEOISIE. He didn't have much love for the proletariat either, even though he was a paid-up Communist for a while. Basically, he hated people: 'I feel no relationship with this human stew,' he said. His need to vent spleen was more personal than political, a deep-seated aesthetic disgust with his fellow man. But his misanthropic images were appreciated in 1920s Berlin as biting satirical commentary, and they resonate in retrospect as an expression of a time and place. He was a fine draughts-man and one of the most effective wielders of caricature as a weapon. What Communism did was to point to a legitimate target for his indiscriminate scorn. It seemed, he said, noble 'to be intolerant upwards and not down-wards'. Lashing and stabbing at the ruling classes, state institutions, German militarists and self-satisfied philis-tines, he looked like a front-line fighter for the Cause. But his eye was too clear. A visit to Stalin's USSR just showed him more of the same: functionaries who 'seemed like red-covered pamphlets', who 'would actually have been glad to have grey cardboard discs for faces'. He saw what no attacking satirist should — the other side of the coin, and it caused him in time to view his own art as hollow.

He liked to say he left Germany of his own accord, but he was high up on the Nazi blacklist. In America he disappointed people by playing down his past work and attempting a fresh start drawing landscapes. He returned to live in Germany, but was found dead in his cellar after only a few weeks, having fallen down the stairs after a night of drunken bingeing.

"When Hitler came, the feeling came over me like that of a boxer; I felt as if I had lost. All our efforts were for nothing"

JOHN HEARTFIELD

born Berlin
Germany
1891
died Berlin
Germany
1968

"It is our task to influence the masses, as well, as strongly, as intensely as possible**"**

HELMUT HERZFELDE WAS TINY but talented, and is revered by photomontagists as the first and greatest of them all. He anglicised his name to John Heartfield during World War I, as a pacifist gesture, and joined the German Communist Party as soon as it was formed in 1918, along with George Grosz and Erwin Piscator. Under Grosz's influence Heartfield destroyed most of his previous artwork, considering it anaemic. They both dabbled in Dada – a Monty Pythonesque eruption of artistic anarchy, which was also sharply political, particularly in Berlin. Montage, with its rearrangement of 'real' items in unexpected juxtaposition, was a Dadaist sort of thing; but Heartfield was essentially a political cartoonist, and he positioned every item with intent, to convey a clear message. Some, like ***Blood and Iron*** – four bloody axes tied together to make a swastika – have an iconic simplicity. One of his first pieces was disturbingly prescient in 1924: ***After Ten Years: Fathers and Sons*** showed young cadets marching, commanded by a moustached general and overlooked by the skeletons of the World War I generation. Hung in the window of Malik Verlag, the gallery/publishing house he ran with his brother, it attracted crowds and controversy.

He never flinched from attacking the 'enemies of the people', even when under dire threat from the Nazis. After SA troopers raided his home, he fled to Prague and continued producing and publishing his work. When Hitler demanded his extradition in 1938, he flew to London, where he designed book jackets and bred rabbits in Highgate until the war's end.

KURT SCHWITTERS

born Hanover
Germany
1887
died Kendal
England
1948

SOME MODERN ART IS RUBBISH, as we all know. Take Schwitters, for example: tirelessly recycling worthless detritus — tram tickets, dishcloths, shoelaces, wire, feathers, cheese-wrappers, cigar bands, fag ends, bits of wood, torn newspaper and photographs — to make his collages, assemblages and sculptures. He was a 24-hour-a-day artist, who travelled with two huge portfolios from which he sold collages at 20 marks each. 'A totally free spirit; he was ruled by Nature,' remembered his fellow Dadaist Hans Richter. The Dada movement as such rejected him for having a 'bourgeois face', but even if his politics didn't fit, the earnestness of his absurdity was true Dada. Unfazed by rejection, he formed a one-man artistic movement: *Merz*, he called it, from a fragment of type in a Commerzbank advert that found its way into one of his collages. He drew Merz, sculpted Merz, recited Merz at his poetry soirées (the assemblage principle worked for words too) and he even called himself Merz.

In his Hanover house he built his 'Merzbau', a walk-through installation with nooks and crannies, angular protuberances, and objects everywhere that were being added to constantly. A central 'column of erotic misery' rose up until it went through the ceiling, necessitating the eviction of the top-floor tenants (no problem: Schwitters was the landlord).

The Nazis thought he should be locked up. They confiscated what they could of his works, but Schwitters himself escaped to Norway, where he started a new Merzbau. Then, when the Germans arrived there too, he fled to Britain. Here, in its wisdom, the government decided that the best thing to do with the thousands of arriving refugees — escapees from Nazi persecution — was to round them up and put them in a camp on the Isle of Man. 'Collar the lot!' said Churchill, though, in fact, only half the 50,000 or so Germans were interned, and most of them not for long. One of the 'collared' was Schwitters, and he whiled away the detention drawing portraits of fellow internees, just as others gave physics or language lessons, or formed string quartets.

He lived out his last years in a quiet corner of the Lake District, building a third Merzbau in a disused straw barn near Ambleside. The first Merzbau, in Hanover, was destroyed in an air raid. The second, in Norway, was burnt down. The final construction, unfinished at the time of his death (though no Merzbau could ever really be considered 'finished'), was later reinstalled at the Hatton Gallery in Newcastle.

Schwitters left his mark on art in the second half of the 20th century. By following his instincts he became a pioneer of things like audio art, pop art, performance art, free typography and site-specific installation.

"Everything is right and so is the opposite"

with apologies

69

PABLO PICASSO

born Malaga

Spain

1881

died Mougins

France

1973

EITHER HITLER OR PICASSO was going to take 20th-century culture by the scruff of the neck. Thankfully, ultimately, it was Picasso, and he was a force, above all, for liberation. This he celebrated most exuberantly in 1946 after the Nazi defeat, by painting *La Joie de Vivre*, a merry effusion of his regular motifs of music, dancing, mythical creatures, sensual female forms and sunshine. In choosing to stay in his Paris studio through most of the occupation, Picasso showed not so much bravery as trust in his almost sacred celebrity to keep him safe. The Gestapo made do with occasionally searching his premises and forbidding any exhibitions. Where he showed most bravery was in his art, wrestling with the extremes of his vision, and thereby achieving iconoclastic breakthroughs in visual language. With *Les Demoiselles d'Avignon* (1907), which evolved out of over a hundred preliminary paintings and sketches, he wrenched figurative art into the 20th century at around the same time as Einstein's theories and Stravinsky's *Rite of Spring* were doing the same for physics and music.

'Those who are concerned with the judgements of posterity cannot be free,' he said, showing marked contrast to Hitler, whose crabbed artistic viewpoint could only recognise past values and his own glorious destiny, and who saw this new art as 'spiritual lunacy' and the sign of the beginning of 'the backward development of the human brain'. Did not Hitler recognise in Picasso the nemesis of his own artistic vision? His 'degenerate' status must have been obvious: the supreme individualism that made him such a fertile innovator; the Spaniard's innate anarchism; his pacifism; his association with Jews, including his mistress Dora Maar. And, of course, his art. Surely there was something perverse about someone with such a talent for drawing, wilfully distorting the world he saw and embracing disturbing influences from primitive cultures...

It is ironic that while the many women he loved had to swallow fearfully distorted versions of themselves in his paintings, his portrait of Stalin is positively courteous. Fundamentally a hedonist, it took extreme events in his homeland — the bombing of Guernica, particularly — to brush Picasso with politics, and his subsequent uncritical embrace of Communism was more in the spirit of liberation than of any dogma.

The shocks he gave the world, with the distortions and dislocations of Cubism, have simmered down over time. But *Guernica* remains as powerful as ever, an eternal monument to human suffering, and all the stronger for resisting polemic in favour of Picasso's highly personal symbols — the bull, the horse. Legend has it that a Nazi officer, searching his studio, pointed to one of the preliminary sketches and said 'Did you do that?' To which our hero replied, 'No, *you* did.'

"I don't search, I find"

70

71

MARC CHAGALL

born Vitebsk
Belarus
1887
died St-Paul-de-Vence
France
1985

SON OF A HERRING PICKLER, eldest of nine, whose Hassidic childhood in a Russian *shtetl* provided the inspiration for his nostalgic, unworldly style of painting. He overcame anti-Semitic restrictions to get a good education in St Petersburg that enabled him to paint, play violin, and speak Russian rather than Yiddish. In 1910 he arrived in Paris, the artistic centre of Europe, where he lived and worked for several years, and flirted with Cubism. He was back in Russia by 1917, when the revolution gave citizens' rights at last to Russian Jews, and Chagall was made Fine Arts Commissar for Vitebsk. He embraced the new order enthusiastically, but soon found his artistic individualism hopelessly out of kilter with the comrades. Returning to Paris, he built on his reputation until the Nazis invaded, and then moved his family to unoccupied Provence. There, Varian Fry, from the Emergency Rescue Committee, visited his studio several times, patiently persuading him that as a Jew, not even his celebrity could stave off mortal danger, and his best hope was to get to America. 'Are there cows in America?' he asked, reluctant to uproot himself from the landscape he loved.

In New York, Chagall designed the costumes and set for Stravinsky's ballet *The Firebird*, and had a hugely successful exhibition at the Museum of Modern Art. After the war he settled again in France. His painting had now lost all of its Cubist hard edges, but the stock of personal images remained as ever: fiddlers, rabbis, lovers, animals, sometimes floating above village huts.

'When Chagall paints,' said Picasso, 'you do not know whether he is asleep or awake. Somewhere or other inside his head there must be an angel.'

"Great art picks up where nature ends"

OTTO DIX

born
Untermhaus
Germany
1891
died
Singen
Germany
1969

IF DIX SCOWLED AS FIERCELY all the time as he did whenever he painted self-portraits, he would have suffered serious headaches. Maybe he did. It was the frown of an intense observer, determined to record 'the strongest impression of actuality', whether that be the activity of worms on the corpse of a dead sentry or the effect of gravity on large breasts. In the Weimar Republic years he was the prime artist of the New Objectivity movement, a visual chronicler of Berlin's streets, cabarets and brothels, with paintings like his triptych **Big City**. The Nazis dismissed him without notice from his professorship at the Dresden Art Academy. Some of his pictures, they cited, injured German moral sensibilities; others 'could dampen the will of the German people to defend themselves'— a reference to his mud-and-guts portrayals of the horrors of war, born out of his 1914—18 service as a machine-gunner.

He lay low through the Nazi years, painting empty landscapes which his excellent technique easily handled, but which stood oddly alongside his usual canvases that teemed with human activity. 'I need the tie to the sensual world,' he said, 'the courage to depict ugliness, undiluted life.' He had a compulsion to portray prostitutes, not erotically, but graphically; few artists have drawn such a variety of mammary forms. An unblinking voyeurism and natural bent towards carica-ture make these pictures discomforting. Caricature also gives a bite to his excellent portraits. Several who approached him to be painted lost their nerve and opted out: he was, after all, an ex-machine-gunner.

"You have to see things the way they are. You have to be able to say yes to the human manifestations that exist and will always exist**"**

73

MAX BECKMANN

born Leipzig
Germany
1884
died New York
USA
1950

THE FUNCTION OF ART, said Hitler, 'is not to remind mankind of its deterioration, but rather to counteract it with the eternally beautiful and healthy'. Max Beckmann didn't quite see it like that. 'I try to capture the terrible, thrilling monster of life's vitality and to confine it, to beat it down and to strangle it with crystal-clear, razor-sharp lines and planes,' he explained. Horrible things happen in a Beckmann picture: rape, torture, hands being chopped off, people failing to meet each other's eyes. His overcrowded canvases portray cramped, angular interiors in which haunted, anguished figures are defined in flat colour and strong black outline. He believed a painting should be 'an individual, organic, universal whole', which might contain almost anything, and offer a narrative to be read on several levels. Often he drew himself, a fierce, brooding presence, not at all eternally beautiful or healthy. In paintings, lithographs and dry points he portrayed an inner world, too introspective to be blatantly political, but still part of the New Objectivity tendency towards 'real' scenes with an undercurrent of social criticism. It was the work of a sensitive and bruised soul, traumatised by his World War I experiences as a medic, yet an ambitious man who wanted to compete with Matisse and Picasso on their home ground.

All was going fine for him until his work offended the sensitivities of Hitler. Within months of taking power, the Nazis had him dismissed from his Frankfurt teaching post. Around six hundred of his works were removed from German museums and nine were then included in the Degenerate Art Exhibition. On the opening day of that exhibition, after hearing Hitler's radio speech about the 'gruesome malfunctioning of the artists' eyes', Beckmann and his wife fled Germany for ever. For almost a decade they lived in Amsterdam, seeking respite from the horrors of war by visits to the theatre, concerts and carnivals, details of which he translated into his pictures. This was his most productive period. After the war he moved to the USA, where he was well respected — though, as a figurative painter, unfashionable in the new age of avant-garde abstraction. He has been called 'a father-figure without progeny', representing both climax and conclusion of his school of painting. He was revered as a teacher, despite a lack of English that required his wife to attend his classes as translator — usually carrying their Pekinese dog, Butschy. For power of imagery and the feeling conveyed in his pictures of being near the dark heart of an extreme time, he was perhaps the greatest 20th-century German painter. He died in New York of a cardiac arrest while walking to the Metropolitan Museum of Art, to see his work in the exhibition American Painting Today.

"Everything intellectual and transcendent is joined together in painting by the uninterrupted labour of the eyes"

75

MAX ERNST

born Brühl
Germany
1891
died Paris
France
1976

CULTIVATED, INTELLECTUAL, a student of philosophy and psychiatry rather than art. Though a leading light of both Dada and Surrealism, he resisted absolute identification with these movements, just as he distanced his conscious self from his own pictures ('I came to exist as a spectator at the birth of all my works'). He was always experimenting with new techniques — montage, collage, decalcomania (squidging paint against glass), grattage (scraping away different-coloured layers of dry paint) and particularly frottage (making rubbings over textured surfaces like floorboards) — letting the actual subject matter rise from his subconscious as a true Surrealist should. What then bubbled up from below were shadowy forest landscapes, luxuriant and menacing, overseen by strange moons. And a gothic cast of disturbing forms: hybrids — part human, part bird, part machine; fantasy creatures like the curious 'Lop-Lop' — half bird, half easel.

A particularly nightmarish and apocalyptic creature rampages across his 1937 picture series **Angel of Hearth and Home**, one of his most dynamic images, created in a rare response to political events. Generally, he was inclined to place forms in his pictures statically, as if they were sculptures. In fact some of his best pieces were actual sculptures — like **Capricorn**, which

"A painter is lost if he finds himself**"**

76

gives a good idea of what a surrealist family might look like, should you ever meet one.

From 1922 Ernst lived in France and, as a German national, was interned at the outbreak of war. After release he was re-arrested and interned again when the Germans invaded. His name was on a list of 2500 inmates whose lives were considered in danger should the Nazis reach the camp, and were thus evacuated by train. He made his way to Varian Fry's villa near Marseilles, where he found his old friend André Breton ensconced, hosting merry evenings for stranded Surrealists. While waiting there for papers, he improvised a tree-hung exhibition outside.

Another improvised exhibition, at the Spanish border, helped him out of France after officials deemed his passport invalid and were about to send him by train back to imprisonment. 'Monsieur, I adore talent,' said the French stationmaster, pointedly adding, as he returned the passport and turned his back, that Ernst must be careful not to take the wrong train.

In Spain he was joined by the bohemian art collector Peggy Guggenheim, who had been working with Fry to rescue artists. She flew with Ernst to the USA, and after another internment – in Ellis Island – she became his third wife for a while. Other wives and lovers included fellow painters Leonora Carrington and Dorothea Tanning, singer/actress Lotte Lenya, and Paul Eluard's wife Gala – who later became Salvador Dali's mistress and muse. Ernst's first wife, the Jewish journalist Luise Straus, was murdered in Auschwitz.

FELIX NUSSBAUM

born Osnabrück
Germany
1904
died Auschwitz
Poland
1944

"If I perish, don't let my paintings die. Show them to people"

'A MESSAGE IN A BOTTLE' is what architect Daniel Libeskind calls Nussbaum's paintings. Saved by a dentist, they are now in the Felix Nussbaum Museum – Libeskind's first completed building – in Osnabrück. Felix and his partner, Felka, were refugees from the moment they heard, in Rome, that the Nazis had come to power. They settled in Brussels and got married. Meanwhile, when Jewish businesses were outlawed in 1937, his brother fled Germany for the Netherlands, to be joined by his parents after *Kristallnacht* saw the Osnabrück synagogue burnt down and Jews sent to Dachau.

When Belgium and France fell in 1940, Felix was transported to an internment camp near the Pyrenees. In despair he applied to return to Germany and managed in the process to escape on the Brussels train instead. Reunited with Felka, he was now a fugitive, in hiding without papers; but friends provided him with a studio and art materials. He painted persistently throughout his exile, pictures that show a fine technique and an increasing sense of horror. Works like his haunting **Self-portrait with Jewish Star and Identity Card**, besides keeping something of himself alive, relate a story which belonged to countless Jews.

In 1943, ten years of eluding capture ended. Felix and Felka were arrested and sent to Auschwitz. So were his parents, his brother and his brother's family. Within a couple of months they were all dead.

BRUNO SCHULZ

born Drogobych
Galicia
1892
died Drogobych
Poland
1942

"Poetry happens when short circuits of sense occur between words, a sudden regeneration of the primaeval myths**"**

POLISH-JEWISH GRAPHIC ARTIST and writer, whom John Updike has called 'one of the greatest transmogrifiers of the world into words'. And, one might add, into pictures. An original beyond categorisation, he created a sensual inner world of memories and dreams. He worked as a schoolteacher, filling any spare time with writing, drawing, etching and lithography. His first book of stories was published at 40: **Cinnamon Shops**, which in time found fame in the USA as **Streets of Crocodiles**. This and another couple of books comprise his total published output, though he reputedly wrote something called *The Messiah* which has not yet turned up, and he may also have translated Kafka's *The Trial* into Polish.

Apart from when he studied architecture in Lvov and fine arts in Vienna, he rarely saw the need to leave his home town of Drogobych. His many pictures, mostly monochrome drawings and lithographs, have a Kafkaesque feel: Drogobych is often the setting for dream scenes populated by dominating women and masochistic men (some of whom resemble the artist). In 1939 the town was overrun and occupied by Soviet troops, who were superseded by the Nazis in 1941. One Gestapo officer took to Schulz's art and offered him protection, including passes out of the ghetto and commissions to paint murals. This same officer killed a Jewish dentist who had been receiving protection from another officer. In retaliation, that other officer shot Bruno Schulz in the street as he was bringing bread back into the ghetto.

KÄTHE KOLLWITZ

born Königsberg
East Prussia
1867
died Moritzburg
Germany
1945

"I do not want to die … until I have faithfully made the most of my talent and cultivated the seed that was placed in me until the last small twig has grown**"**

OPPRESSION, POVERTY, DEATH, especially the death of children: these were her subjects, alongside many self-portraits. She lost her own son to World War I and her grandson to World War II, and was often under the cloud of depression. But she and her art enjoyed the affection of ordinary people, as well as commanding a wide respect for the quality of her drawing. Streets and parks were named after her in her lifetime. Though often called an Expressionist, she was more accurately a documentary artist who expressed with lyricism, drama and directness the social conditions in the poor area of Berlin where she lived. Her husband was a doctor and she witnessed the hardship of his patients, many of whom were permanently malnourished. Her drawing was mainly in black and white, using local people as models. She was attracted to print-making because of the possibilities of cheap dissemination of her work, and became highly skilled first in etching, then in lithography and woodcuts.

In 1899, Kaiser Wilhelm II vetoed Kollwitz's receipt of a gold medal at the Berlin Salon because of her subversive subject matter. So it was nothing new to her when the Nazis found her 'bolshevism' intolerable and forbade her to exhibit. They confiscated a number of her works from museums and forced her out of her position as the first female professor appointed to the Prussian Academy of Art. But she was left alone to continue living and working in Berlin — until the British bombed her home in 1943 and she was evacuated.

VICKY (VICTOR WEISZ)

born Berlin
Germany
1913
died London
England
1966

AS THE NAZI SHADOW lengthened, a young Jew of Hungarian origin arrived in London with a peculiar skill. Brought up in Berlin, he had kept his family since his teens by drawing cartoons and illustrations. His potential was recognised by the *News Chronicle*, who paid him a retainer while he educated himself in the essentials of British culture — Dickens, cricket, Lewis Carroll — emerging to become, arguably, Britain's greatest 20th-century cartoonist. He was acutely political, with a wry humour, and a wispy style that he could vary to suit shades of subject matter. Like David Low, he applied brush lines and ink wash to conventional subjects, such as his scene of Churchill and Roosevelt wooing a bescarfed female Stalin, under the spell of a nearby cupid who is Hitler, armed with a quiver of arrows marked 'the common danger' (1941). Later he used restless penstrokes alongside blocks of black, as when, after the Gary Powers incident, he drew the mid-air collision between a U2 rocket and the dove of peace above the 1960 summit conference. Vicky was no cynical hack: he had believed in that summit. He wore his political heart on his sleeve, but with irony and charm. For subjects like poverty or the Holocaust, where caricature would be inappropriate, he slipped into what he called his 'Oxfam style', reminiscent of Käthe Kollwitz. In lighter penstrokes he mocked Macmillan — whom he sent up as unflappable 'Supermac' in the *Evening Standard* — Khrushchev, Kennedy, Adenauer and de Gaulle. He often appeared himself as a tiny, baffled figure alongside them. Some of his best cartoons were in the *New Statesman*, his spiritual home, and with its editor, Kingsley Martin, Vicky joined Bertrand Russell, James Cameron and Michael Foot in the vanguard of the Campaign for Nuclear Disarmament.

His genius was a finely balanced combination of personal qualities over and above the drawing skill. 'You must have pity as well as anger, passion and compassion, hatred and love. That's why a political cartoonist is a very rare bird.' But the relentlessness, the knowledge and acceptance that few cartoons survive for more than a day, that tomorrow always starts with a blank sheet of paper, put a terrible strain on him. He was a worrier — 'a perfectionist in need of endless reassurance', according to his journalist friend James Cameron — and insomnia plagued him. As a romantic socialist he felt deeply disappointed by Wilson's Labour government. For whatever reason, despair overcame him, and he killed himself with an overdose of his regular sleeping pills.

"If readers do not complain, you have not got a cartoonist! My job is to tread on people's toes"

80

81

PAUL RENNER

born Wernigerode

Prussia

1878

died Munich

Germany

1956

"Political idiocy, growing more violent and malicious every day, may eventually sweep the whole of western culture to the ground with its muddy sleeve**"**

THE PHYSICAL IDEAL of Aryan manhood, a true 'Siegfried' with his blond hair and chiselled profile, Renner was an eminent type designer, the highly respected director of the Meisterschule in Munich. A serious intellectual who sought balance between innovation and continuity; a man with a very Prussian sense of duty and suspicion of modern fads like jazz, cinema and abstract art. Yet he was responsible for **Futura**, a typeface as modern as it was possible to be while remaining functional. (The font you're reading now is Futura Condensed — *see* p.iv.) In the spirit of the age of beautiful machines, Futura is stripped of human quirks, including serifs and most of the calligraphic features that propel text forward — such as the curve at the bottom of a 't'. He made ascenders slightly taller than the capitals in order to play down the excess of capitals in German text.

In 1932 Renner published a booklet, **Cultural Bolshevism?**, a carefully argued criticism of the Nazi anti-Semitic and anti-Communist rhetoric that damned Modernism. In response the Nazis started harassing him, and arrested him in April 1933. A concrete charge was hard to pin on him, partly because there was no clear Nazi ideology relating to graphic design. Evidence of photomontage found in his studio was deemed 'communistic', and Futura, with its aura of internationalism, was linked to the 'bolshevist' Bauhaus style of modern architecture. A family contact with Rudolf Hess got him released, but he was dismissed from his job for being 'nationally untrustworthy'. He left for Switzerland and concentrated on painting.

JACQUES LIPCHITZ

born Druskieniki
Lithuania
1891
died Capri
Italy
1973

'I WAS KILLING HITLER through my sculpture,' said Lipchitz, referring to the nine-metre-high **Prometheus Strangling the Vulture**, the piece that he was commissioned to make for the 1937 Paris World Fair (where Picasso's *Guernica* was also exhibited). Other sculptures he produced around this time include **David and Goliath** in which Goliath, wearing a swastika on his chest, is strangled by David; and **The Rape of Europa**, showing Europa stabbing her Hitleresque defiler. If the Nazis still hadn't got the message, there was also the sculptor's Jewishness to bear in mind. He may, even so, have hoped that fame would protect him, as it seemed to protect his friend Picasso, who was left unharmed in Paris throughout the German occupation.

Born in Lithuania, Chaim Jacob Lipchitz arrived in Paris at the age of 18 and joined the artistic avant-garde. Besides Picasso, he befriended Braque and Modigliani (who painted him), and was soon considered Cubism's number one sculptor. African art, which he collected, also influenced his work.

As certainty of his fate in Nazi hands became clear to him, he moved down to the unoccupied South, keeping a supply of poison to hand in case of capture. It was Varian Fry from the Emergency Rescue Committee whose persistent warnings and offers of help persuaded him that flight to America might just be a better fate than poison. He went reluctantly, with no knowledge of English, taking only two of his sculptures. When he got there he loved it, calling his arrival an injection of youth at the beginning of his artistic maturity.

"Art is an action against death. It is a denial of death**"**

83

ERICH MENDELSOHN

born Allenstein

Germany

1887

died San Francisco

USA

1953

MASTER OF ROUNDED CORNERS, the grandfather of Modernist architecture, always seeking to unite the spiritual with the functional. Despite returning wounded from World War I and then losing his left eye to cancer, his most productive decade was the 1920s. He built Berlin's first reinforced concrete villa, several large department stores, and the remarkable **Einstein Tower** in Potsdam – an observatory designed to test the Theory of Relatvity. Germany should have been proud of him; but he was Jewish.

In 1933 he moved to England, where he changed his name from Erich to Eric, and in partnership with ex-ballroom dancer Serge Chermayeff built hospitals and gave the country its first multistorey car park. His design for the **De La Warr Pavilion** on Bexhill seafront, with its spectacular spiral staircase in a glazed cylinder, was one of Britain's first Modernist masterpieces.

He also turned his attention to Palestine, attracted by 'the union of the most modern civilisation and a most antique culture'. His work there included the **Hebrew University** and **Hadassah Hospital** in Jerusalem, the **Villa Weizmann** in Rehovot, and various projects in Tel Aviv (dubbed 'Bauhaus-by-the-Sea' due to the popularity of that most distinctive style of architecture).

From 1941 he lived in the USA, where his reputation was eclipsed. While Frank Lloyd Wright made the architectural headlines and Gropius designed skyscrapers that were high profile in every way, Mendelsohn busied himself with hospitals and synagogues.

"Function without a sensual component remains construction"

the bauhaus

In parallel with the republic there was born in Weimar a radical enterprise that influenced architecture, art and design across the world and throughout the 20th century, thanks to the diaspora created by Hitler's persecution of its practitioners. In 1919, the architect Walter Gropius was appointed to head both the Fine Arts Academy and the Crafts School in Weimar. He combined them into one institution, the Bauhaus (literally, building-house). The chaos of war's aftermath meant damaged buildings, administrative turmoil and lack of both money and facilities; but it was also a window of opportunity for innovation unhampered by the *status quo*. Gropius plunged into action with a clear new vision for art education. The initial slogan was 'art and craft – a new unity', and this was to become 'art and technology – a new unity', as Gropius dragged art, kicking and screaming, into the age of machines and mass production. Staff were called 'masters', students were 'apprentices', the best of whom could become 'journeymen'. Women, newly emancipated by the republic's constitution, were keen applicants, though they were usually nudged towards the weaving workshop. Other workshops included metal, ceramics, architecture, theatre, typography, furniture and photography. The Bauhaus liked to market its products: it was true to the 'useful art' ideology, and helped them a little way in the direction of financial independence.

The Nazis viewed the Bauhaus's emphasis on primary colours and simple, geometric forms, including square buildings, as a regression towards a primitive, racially inferior style. They also, with more justification, suspected bolshevism was involved: a number of apprentices were Communist Party members and Hannes Meyer, who took over as director when Gropius moved on in 1928, was a Marxist.

For subsidy, the Bauhaus was always at the mercy of local government. Thuringia, where Weimar is located, was the first region in which the Nazis came to share political control. The school moved hastily to Dessau, and later to Berlin, but as the Nazis marched into power, the Bauhaus, like the republic, was doomed.

WALTER GROPIUS

born Berlin
Germany
1883
died Boston
USA
1969

'GENEROUS', 'NOBLE', 'CIVILISED', 'handsome', 'touchingly kind', 'a gentleman'... so Alma Mahler described Gropius after divorcing him and making sure she had custody of their child. Their affair during her marriage to Mahler had sent the composer to Freud for counselling. Mahler died on Gropius's birthday: the sort of coincidence that Alma always thought significant. A few years later, she looked up Gropius again and married him in between her affairs with Kokoschka and Werfel. It can't have helped that he was in the army, fighting World War I, through much of their marriage.

His was the vision, dedication and energy behind the Bauhaus. As a leader, he forged a strong sense of community and shared responsibility. He was tireless in his advocacy: lobbying, writing and lecturing on the school's behalf. Most of his effort was spent in fighting opposition, chiefly at the local political level.

As an architect he was so influential that his revolutionary designs have now come to look routine. Typical, with their white walls and clean horizontal lines, was the cluster of houses, each with a studio, built for the Bauhaus masters. Thanks to the structural role taken by steel and ferroconcrete, Gropius was able to conceive walls as mere climate barriers; he was one of the first to use walls of glass. His approach led the way — for good or bad — to prefabrication, housing estates, and all those flat-roofed little boxes that proliferated after the war.

"The ultimate aim of all creative activity is the building"

LYONEL FEININGER

born New York
USA
1871
died New York
USA
1956

"Bach has been my master in painting. I consider my drawings and sketches as melodies, the completed painting, organised and orchestrated in colour, like a large-scale composition for the organ or orchestra**"**

SON OF GERMAN VIOLINIST CARL, and father of American photographer Andreas, Lyonel Feininger started and ended his life in New York, but spent 49 of his 85 years in Germany. He arrived in Hamburg as a music student, but soon switched to art. His early professional years were spent as a caricaturist and strip cartoonist for both German and American newspapers, an apprenticeship in the discipline of drawing and meeting deadlines that he believed provided the best of his art training. From 1907 he evolved into a painter and print-maker, with a distinctive Cubist style, full of angular lines and planes in rhythmic arrangement. He was a member of the *Blaue Reiter* group, and his reputation was well established when Gropius appointed him as a 'master' in the first year of the Bauhaus.

His woodcut **Cathedral of Socialism**, with beams of light picking out the three spires that symbolised painting, sculpture and architecture, was printed in the Bauhaus manifesto. Its modernist zest did much to attract the 150 students who initially enrolled. He was not one for systematic theory and declined to give formal classes, preferring a role of artist-in-residence and considering his job was not to teach, but to 'help create an atmosphere'. He looked askance at the shift towards sales and mass production that came in 1922, but acknowledged Gropius's pragmatism in attempting to free the Bauhaus from financial dependence on the state. He stayed until the end, eventually leaving in 1937 (his wife was Jewish) for New York. Nineteen of his pictures were in the Degenerate Art Exhibition.

VASSILY KANDINSKY

born Moscow

Russia

1866

died Neuilly-sur-Seine

France

1944

THE ORIGINAL MISTER ABSTRACT, founding father of non-figurative art, who abandoned a legal career to take up painting at the age of 30. He was an initiator and teacher and an influential theorist through his book **Concerning the Spiritual in Art**. His ideas were too subjective and spiritual for post-revolutionary Russia, and he left for Berlin.

He was an egocentric mystic with a hypersensitivity to the expressive qualities of colour: he 'heard' colour, much as his fellow Russian synaesthete, the composer Scriabin, 'saw' sound. (Yellow 'sounds like a trumpet'; violet:'sickly and sad'.) Kandinsky played the cello and piano, and his paintings often took musical titles (eg *Composition, Improvisation*). This musical inclination no doubt made it easier for him to move painting into abstraction, but, like his composing friend Schoenberg, the pioneer of atonalism, he felt the weight of historical responsibility on him. 'What is to replace the missing object?' he asked himself. Critics were unable to see any sense behind what seemed an involuntary conglomeration of colours. He co-founded the influential *Blaue Reiter* group, organised a number of international avant-garde exhibitions and taught at the Bauhaus from 1922. There he settled as head of the mural-painting workshop, finding kindred spirits in Klee and Feininger, respect from students, and the chance to set out the theoretical basis of 'non-objective composition' in his book **Point and Line to Plane**.

Being Russian and an abstractionist — what a German newspaper called 'an insane painter who can no longer be held responsible for his actions' — clinched his 'undesirable' status for the Nazis. In the Degenerate Art Exhibition, one of his works was annotated 'crazy at any price'. The Bauhaus job on its own was enough to make him 'bolshevist', even though, as escapees from the real Bolsheviks, the Kandinskys fitted uncomfortably into the leftist politics of the school. (His wife Nina is said to have fainted at the sight of a red flag.)

In 1933, he decamped to Paris, where he was disconcerted to find his work was hardly known, abstraction being regarded as a development of French Cubism. He supposed his exile to be temporary, and did not greatly engage with his new milieu. Always naïve about the political world around him, he wrote to the Nazi authorities to stress his German citizenship, and that he was 'only in Paris for reasons of his art'. But he never returned.

"Colour is the keyboard, the eyes are the harmonies, the soul is the piano with many strings. The artist is the hand that plays, touching one key or another, to cause vibrations in the soul"

89

PAUL KLEE

born Münchenbuchsee
Switzerland
1879
died Muralto
Switzerland
1940

THE BAUHAUS BUDDHA. Uncategorisable Swiss artist whose work explored the primary elements of line and colour in a most original manner, combining childlike freedom and whimsy with intellectual, rather mystical theorising, honed in his years as 'master of form' at the Bauhaus. His pictures grew in a dreamlike way out of basic processes. He talked of 'letting a point wander through space', or 'taking a line for a walk'; or he constructed a grid of coloured squares — all exercises in the abstract into which might then drift wisps of figurative meanings: a face, a plant, a village. Such doodlings brought forth a body of almost 10,000 pictures which, through their combined sophistication and playfulness, have since engaged a wide following, even amongst a public sceptical of modern art.

In 1911 he met Kandinsky and other members of the *Blaue Reiter*, with whom he exhibited in 1912. Drafted into the German army in 1915, he spent much of the war painting camouflage on aircraft. His fame broadened during his Bauhaus years, with major exhibitions in Berlin and the New York Museum of Modern Art.

The son of musicians, he married a musician and played the violin himself. Like Feininger and Kandinsky, he had a musical approach to painting, conjuring up a private dreamworld with an improvisatory lyricism. This was seen by the Nazis to be clear evidence of mental retardation, and in the Degenerate Art Exhibition 17 of his pictures were displayed alongside drawings by mentally ill people, with an encouragement to the viewer to spot the difference. His statement 'I cannot be grasped in the here and now, for I live just as well with the dead as with the unborn' was used in the exhibition to mock him. Many of his paintings were withdrawn from German museums and later sold abroad in exchange for foreign currency.

In 1931 he resigned from the Bauhaus and started teaching at the State Art Academy in Düsseldorf. His house was searched by the Nazis in 1933 and he was challenged to provide proof of his Aryan descent — which he failed to do. A local paper called him 'a Siberian *Ostjude* and dangerous *Kulturbolschewist*'. His best student turned informer and he fled Düsseldorf for his homeland, settling with his wife in artistic isolation near Locarno. But he died before his Swiss citizenship was granted. He developed scleroderma, a disease that slowly mummified him, and his last years saw him completely immersed in producing paintings — larger than before and with broader strokes. Working with both hands, in a desperate race against time, his output grew to over 1200 pieces in the last full year of his life.

"Let art sound like a fairy tale and be at home everywhere. Let it work with good and evil as do the eternal powers"

91

MARCEL BREUER

born Pécs
Hungary
1902
died New York
USA
1981

"They get better and better ... in the end you'll be sitting on an elastic column of air**"**

THE FUTURE IS TUBULAR. This was the revelation granted to Marcel Breuer, as he contemplated the handlebars on his bicycle. He was the man behind all those wonderful, neat, minimal chairs that still feel modern 75 years on, with their geometrical tubular frames of bent steel piping, welded and cantilevered, fleshed out with plain strips of fabric, and all somehow moulded to your body's natural sitting style.

A Bauhaus student who was promoted to master of furniture, his design philosophy was exemplary – minimum weight (including 'visual' weight) and maximum strength: the 'minimax solution'. Earlier Bauhaus efforts at a cantilevered steel tubing chair had been rigid and uncomfortable. Breuer's insight was to use steel that was not reinforced, and therefore had a bit of give. His breakthrough chair was called the ***Wassily***, made for his colleague Kandinsky, and he continued to refine the concept in the many variations that followed, looking for lighter weight, and that irresistible, gentle bouncing quality. 'I always aimed,' he said, to find 'the last solution.'

The Nazis, also interested in 'last solutions', made sure he didn't sit comfortably for long. He followed Gropius, first to England in 1935, then to the USA, where they shared an architectural business. Later, he became a Harvard professor of architecture. His buildings include the ***Whitney Museum of American Art*** in New York and the ***UNESCO HQ*** in Paris.

His favourite colour: white – 'there is seldom a reason to replace it with any other colour.'

LASZLO MOHOLY-NAGY

born Bacsborsod
Hungary
1895
died Chicago
USA
1946

'LIKE A STRONG, EAGER DOG' (said his wife), this enthusiastic 28-year-old Hungarian 'burst into the Bauhaus and … attacked its unresolved tradition-bound problems'. He spearheaded the move towards greater unity between art and technology, taking over the *Vorkurs* (foundation course) and virtually dropping drawing from the curriculum while the students built little 3-D objects out of blocks and spheres. He created a Bauhaus corporate style and encouraged everyone to broaden their familiarity with machines.

Moholy's legacy was to change the understanding of the possibilities of art. He made set designs for the Kroll Opera and Piscator Theatre, and developed a 'theatre of totality', in which scenery, lighting and stage design were elevated to have equal status with actors and their words. He experimented with photograms (camera-free photography) and pioneered kinetic art. He created a **Light Space Modulator** – a motor-driven sculpture lit to cast a rich variety of shadows.

In 1937, he tried to revive the Bauhaus in Chicago, where his idealism came up against hard-nosed industrialists who were not going to sponsor a new school if it was slow to come up with the goods. Though he promised to produce 'art engineers' rather than arty-farty types, the Chicago Bauhaus folded within a year. Moholy concluded ruefully, 'The success theory of the profit economy pays a high premium to the anti-artist.'

"Art is the means by which scientific discovery can be reconciled with human needs and desires**"**

6

Undesirable
music

Nobody in Germany or Austria seriously doubted the superiority of Germanic music. It was the central pillar of the national culture they shared, the measure of the depth of the collective soul. The history of Western composition could self-evidently be seen as a steady ascent led by successive Austro-Germans – Bach, Haydn, Mozart, Beethoven, Wagner. For Hitler, Richard Wagner (an equally monstrous egotist who, incidentally, happened to consider Jewish composers to be 'worms feeding on the body of art') represented an arrival at perfection. Any conceivable attempts to develop the art form further could only be regarded as degeneracy – especially if by a primitive Russian like Stravinsky or, worse, by Jews like Mahler and Schoenberg.

The atonalism of Schoenberg and his pupils was one of the most obvious signs of musical degeneracy. (Another, harder to combat, was jazz; the Nazis rather hoped they could offset this infectious new popular music form by an energetic promotion of national folk music.) Only with the rise of Nazism did Schoenberg embrace and assert his Jewishness: previously he was as chauvinistic about German music as all the rest. In his excursions into atonalism and then Serialism (the method of composition which treats all twelve notes of a scale as equal, instead of favouring the basic doh-mi-soh notes of chords), he was doing what composers have always done: building on, and reacting to, what had gone before. The music of Wagner and Mahler – anti-Semite and Jew – ran equally through his veins, and he believed his achievements were 'assuring the supremacy of German music for the next hundred years'. With his pupils, Berg and Webern, he formed what was known as the Second Viennese School which, like most sequels, failed to live up to the success of the original team of Haydn, Mozart and Beethoven.

In 1936, the world heard that the statue of Mendelssohn, which stood in front of the Leipzig Gewandhaus, had been reduced to rubble. Thus the assimilated Jewish composer, a devout Lutheran

timeline

1938

Mar •Germany annexes Austria (the *Anschluss*)

May •Degenerate Music Exhibition in Düsseldorf

Sept •Hitler signs Munich Agreement with Britain and France

Oct •Germany annexes Sudetenland

•Over 17,000 Polish-born Jews expelled from Germany

Nov •*Kristallnacht*. 24 hours of nationwide violence. 91 Jews killed, 30,000 Jews arrested. Thousands of homes broken into. Jews forced to clear up afterwards

1939

Feb •Jews ordered to relinquish all gold and silver

Mar •Germany invades Czechoslovakia

May •Heydrich establishes killing squads and ghettos

Aug •Non-aggression pact signed between Germany and USSR

Sept •Germany invades Poland

•Britain and France declare war

•Radios confiscated from Jews

•Curfew introduced for Jews: 9pm summer, 8pm winter

who did so much to revive the reputation of J.S.Bach, was excised from German musical history. His *Midsummer Night's Dream* music, once evidence of his teenage prodigy, was 'replaced' by an 'Aryanised' version commissioned by the Reich Chamber of Music from a nonentity called Edmund Nick. But in the depths of the Hell that was to come, in faraway Auschwitz, an orchestra of women prisoners, compelled to play for their captors, were to score a secret victory by playing Mendelssohn's violin concerto for their unsuspecting camp guards.

A Degenerate Music Exhibition opened in Düsseldorf in 1938, spelling out the official line on undesirability. But most of those featured had already left the stage: between 1933 and 1939 more than 1500 conductors, soloists, singers, instrumentalists and musicologists were expelled from concert halls and teaching positions throughout Germany and Austria because they were Jewish. Non-Jews, like Erich Kleiber, esteemed director of the Berlin State Opera, joined the exodus in sympathy, and those, such as the composer Richard Strauss and the conductor Wilhelm Furtwängler, who hung on in the belief that their status could shield them from politics, were given an uncomfortable time if they didn't toe the Nazi line.

The Versailles Treaty had expressly forbidden any merging between Austria and Germany into a Greater Germany; yet union was an enduring aspiration for many people in these two lands that already shared both language and culture. When Hitler, with a combination of menace and political skill, achieved *Anschluss* (annexation) in 1938, his entry into Vienna was mainly welcomed with open arms. The Nazis wasted no time: the deposed Chancellor Schuschnigg was the first of 76,000 sent to Dachau concentration camp. Anti-Jewish measures that were already in place in Germany were extended wholesale, and expensive exit permits made obligatory for Jews who wanted to try to leave. Then Hitler ordered a plebiscite and was delighted to be able to say that the people gave his actions an unbelievable 99% approval.

ARNOLD SCHOENBERG

MOSES UNDERSTOOD GOD, but it was Aaron who could speak to the people. Schoenberg, an Austrian Jew who never found a way of ending his opera ***Moses and Aaron***, had his own tablets of stone to deliver, but the people never really took to his message. He believed that, in pursuit of expression, Wagner had stretched harmony as far as it could go: music would now just have to abandon its grip on the tonal system, forget about keys and chords, and dive into atonalism. He took this plunge around the time that his painter friend Kandinsky was taking art into abstraction. (Schoenberg was a painter himself, in a raw expressionist style, and exhibited with the *Blaue Reiter*.)

In 1909 he wrote ***Erwartung***, in which a soprano expresses the fluctuating emotional extremes of a woman searching a forest for her lover: a piece without musical rules, sounding as if it might have poured straight out of the depths of his subconscious on the couch of his Viennese neighbour, Dr Freud. This was followed by ***Pierrot Lunaire***, in which the vocal part was declaimed in something halfway between singing

born Vienna

Austria

1874

died Los Angeles

USA

1951

"I was a conservative who was forced to become a revolutionary; but what I did was neither revolution nor anarchy**"**

and speaking. Then, in 1924, he announced new rules to take the place of those he had abandoned. This was Serialism, the 'twelve-tone theory', and was, in Schoenberg's mind, historically inevitable: *someone* was going to have to do it. For the moment, yes, his new language was hard to grasp, but in ten years (he was often to extend this timescale as the years passed) people would 'find it natural', they would 'know my tunes and whistle them'. But people never thought his tunes *were* tunes. They preferred the sort of thing written by composers like his friend and tennis partner, fellow Jew and fellow painter, George Gershwin.

Schoenberg was clear-sighted enough to get out of Europe in early 1934, eventually settling in Hollywood. Once there, he did more teaching than composing; indeed, he was reputed to be a very good teacher, with intuitive understanding of his students and no wish to subject them to his own interpretations. Yet, to share Schoenberg's friendship, you had to believe in his greatness. His pupils did, and so did Gershwin. But otherwise he perceived enemies everywhere: conductors like Klemperer and Bruno Walter who wouldn't play his works enough or properly; universities that underpaid him for his teaching; anyone who hesitated to accept his Moses-like status. Approached by MGM for film music, he demanded a colossal $50,000 and the right to control the pitch at which the actors spoke. Naturally he lost that commission, and any fame and wealth that would have accompanied it, but his integrity and patriarchal status remained intact.

ANTON WEBERN

born Vienna
Austria
1883
died Mittersill
Austria
1945

"There is no other way**"**

IF LESS IS MORE, then Webern wrote a phenomenal amount of music. Actually, you could hear the whole of his life's work in a single three-hour concert, though it might be a harrowing experience. Distilled into the minimum number of notes, often played by the slimmest of slimmed-down ensembles, was all the emotion of a full symphonic experience. He had a love of nature, and was sometimes to be seen out on the slopes, paying myopic attention to the tiny forms of Alpine flowers. Stravinsky called his pieces 'dazzling diamonds', which suggests the best approach to his music is with the listening equivalent of a jeweller's eyeglass, appreciating the intrinsic qualities of delicate points of sound. For instance, the funeral march of his **Six Orchestral Pieces** starts in near silence, and listening to it with this intensity makes the crescendo that then emerges all the more devastating a reflection of the composer's anguish at his mother's death.

He was attracted to Nazism to begin with, though not when it became a reality; besides, the two composers he most venerated, Mahler and Schoenberg, were Jews. The Nazis certainly didn't care for him: performance of his work was banned, he lost his conducting jobs and was reduced to proof-reading. His daughter married a Nazi; his son died on the Eastern front. Just as the war had ended, and his nerves were recovering, he stepped outside to smoke a cigar and was accidentally killed by a trigger-happy American soldier. He thus missed the chance to hear most of his work actually played, or witness the respect it got from the next generation of composers.

ALBAN BERG

born Vienna
Austria
1885
died Vienna
Austria
1935

"Carnival din, masks and confetti, and on top of that the news of the Reichstag fire. Dancing on a volcano**"**

FEW COUPLES WERE SO DEVOTED as Alban Berg and his wife Helene, (whose mother was allegedly the secret mistress of the Emperor Franz Josef): when apart, they exchanged solicitous letters and phonecalls daily. But Berg also had a 'one and only eternal love', his mistress, Franz Werfel's sister, Hanna. His music was as complex and passionate as his life. He wove intricate ciphers of his love for Hanna into his music, especially the **Lyric Suite**, in which their initials and numbers of private significance are constantly reiterated. (There are artful Berg nerds who have spent decades deciphering this sort of thing.)

Berg followed his teacher Schoenberg into atonalism and Serialism but, unlike Webern, seemed always to be glancing back at Romanticism. This wistfulness gives a poignant charge to pieces like his **Violin Concerto – 'In Memory of an Angel'**, the angel being Manon, the daughter of Alma Mahler and Walter Gropius, who died of polio aged 18. It was Berg's last work: he was stung (or bitten) by an insect, and died of septicaemia at 50, the age at which his idol, Mahler, had died.

Far away in America, Schoenberg had feared that Berg might succumb to Nazism, if only because of the temptation to stress his Aryan pedigree in order to get his works played. Indeed, Berg wrote with resentment that 'since the Berlin Reichstag fire, not a single note of mine has been heard in Germany – although I am not a Jew'. After his death, Helene refused to tout for performances: 'Alban can happily rest until this hell on earth has worked itself out. His time will come.'

VIKTOR ULLMANN

born Teschen
Moravian-Polish border
1898
died Auschwitz
Poland
1944

"We certainly did not sit down by the waters of Babylon and weep**"**

THE CONCENTRATION CAMP called Theresienstadt, in the Czech town Terezín, was a gateway to Hell disguised as a 'Paradise Ghetto'. It was set up by the Nazis as a show camp, to convince the world, via Red Cross inspections, of the humanity of the Nazi treatment of Jews. Inmates comprised a cultural elite – artists, scholars, musicians, scientists – who could be witnessed in camp, painting, writing, putting on operas and educating their children. One, an actor who had appeared with Marlene Dietrich in *Blue Angel*, was commissioned by the Germans to make a film of day-to-day camp life, to be called *The Führer Gives a Village to the Jews*; but within months, both director and cast were dead. Theresienstadt was simply and cynically a transit camp to Auschwitz and other deathcamps.

Viktor Ullmann, a protégé of both Schoenberg and Zemlinsky, composed over 20 works during his two years in Theresienstadt, including songs, piano sonatas, a string quartet and an opera, **The Emperor of Atlantis**. He also organised concerts, gave lectures and ran his Studio for Contemporary Music. 'Our desire for culture was matched by our desire for life,' he wrote. But the Nazis forced the Jewish elders to submit a regular quota of names for transport to Auschwitz, and eventually Ullmann appeared on one of these lists. At the last moment he left his works and diaries with a friend, and they were saved, even if he wasn't.

100

KURT WEILL

born Dessau
Germany
1900
died New York
USA
1950

THE SON OF THE CANTOR at the Dessau synagogue, Weill the composer had a peculiar penchant for the voice, and for the peculiar voice of his wife Lotte Lenya, in particular. If it weren't for the Nazis — who would have considered his music degenerate even had he not been Jewish — he might have had a smooth, rich and successful life in Berlin, building on his early collaborations with Bertolt Brecht, principally **The Threepenny Opera**. This acidic satire, based on John Gay's 1728 *Beggar's Opera*, was performed 4200 times in its first year (1928–29). By 1930, however, the premiere of their **Rise and Fall of the City of Mahagonny** was being assailed by Nazi stinkbombs, and even the optimistic Weill was transferring his royalties to a Swiss bank. When the Nazis took power in 1933 he wrote, 'what is going on now is so sick that I don't know how it can last longer than a few months'. Once they learnt that they were blacklisted, he and Lenya left Germany: Weill for Paris, then England; and

Lenya for Vienna, where she was having one of her countless affairs. At this point they divorced for a while, but she rejoined him when he sailed to New York in 1935, and they remarried.

Weill embraced American culture with enthusiasm, feeling he had 'come home' at last. He was soon networking like a born New Yorker. Despite the difficulties of re-establishing a reputation, he intuitively recognised that the Broadway style was to the American public what the opera houses were to the more elitist Europeans. Weill was a natural populist — though never such a politico as Brecht, and always one to put musical quality before didacticism. When George Gershwin died in 1937, Weill to an extent filled his shoes, even collaborating with his lyricist brother Ira on **Lady in the Dark**. This and subsequent productions made him a household name and his songs were recorded by the likes of Frank Sinatra, Bing Crosby and Count Basie.

As a born-again American, he refused to speak German, and disliked other emigrés, such as Korngold and Adorno. Marlene Dietrich he dismissed as a 'stupid cow, conceited like all Germans'. Many Germans did not forgive him for not returning to his homeland, and European critics still talk of him squandering his talent on Broadway. Likewise, Americans have tended to ignore his Berlin period. To Weill, there were no such boundaries: 'I write for today. I don't give a damn about writing for posterity.' Even so, for years after his rather untimely death, Lenya put a lot of work into making sure posterity gave a damn about Weill.

"In a deeply democratic country like ours, art should belong to the people. It should be 'popular' in the highest sense of the word. Only by making this our aim can we create an American art, as opposed to the art of the old countries"

PAUL HINDEMITH

born Hanau, near Frankfurt
Germany
1895
died Frankfurt
Germany
1963

" I am gradually beginning to feel like a cornerstone on which every passer-by can pass the water of his artistic opinion **"**

IT WAS A MESSY DIVORCE. Neither Hindemith nor Germany really wanted to part from one another. Goebbels, fearing the loss of babies in the draining of musical bathwater, hailed him as 'one of the strongest talents in the younger German generation of composers', but was eventually to denounce him as proof of 'how deeply the Jewish intellectual infection has eaten into the body of our own people'. Goebbels gave way to the implacable Führer who, it seems, could never forgive Hindemith for a scene in his 1929 opera **News of the Day**, in which a soprano sang in a bathtub.

Though never an atonalist (he believed tonality was 'a natural force, like gravity'), Hindemith's early work was outrageous and experimental. He made an Expressionist opera from a text by Kokoschka, and set words by Brecht to something he called 'useful music' — which sounded suspiciously bolshevist. But by the time the Nazis were in power his musical style had mellowed and he was undergoing self-examination as to the responsibilities of an artist in times of political tension: this was the theme of his opera **Mathis der Maler (Matthias the Artist)**. He and the conductor Furtwängler engaged with Goebbels and lost the fight to mount this opera, in the process turning it into a *cause célèbre*. Furtwängler resigned in protest, and Hindemith left the country, albeit late in the day, at first going only as far as Switzerland. Though he later became respected in the USA and postwar Germany as a music educator, his compositions never regained the spark of excitement that is to be found in his youthful works.

HANNS EISLER

born Leipzig
Germany
1898
died Berlin
Germany
1962

ONE OF SCHOENBERG'S most devoted pupils, who nevertheless felt he must turn his back on his master's aesthetic because of his belief that music should have the function of 'usefulness to the people in their struggle'. Eisler came to Berlin in 1925 when the political atmosphere was at its most polarised and feverish, and when the arrival of jazz, sound recording and talking pictures promised new possibilities for a composer, especially if he wanted to reach the masses. Soon he was setting to music the abrasive, satirical texts of Tucholsky and Brecht, and hearing them sung in street demonstrations and left-wing cabarets. **Solidarity Song**, from the 1931 film *Kuhle Wampe (Who Owns the World?)*, became an instant revolutionary hit. The words were by Bertolt Brecht, for whom he proved a more compatible and long-lasting collaborator than did Kurt Weill.

He was lucky to be already out of Germany when Hitler came to power, and after some wandering he settled in Hollywood. Here he renewed his partnership with Brecht, co-writing many songs and a large-scale anti-Fascist **German Symphony**. He also composed some distinguished film music, receiving Oscar nominations in two successive years. The first of these was for his score for **Hangmen Also Die**, Fritz Lang's 1943 film about the death of the Nazi 'Hangman' Heydrich. After the war he was an early and obvious target for the McCarthy witch hunt. He moved to East Berlin, where he composed the music for the GDR national anthem, **Risen from the Ruins**.

"Fascists … cannot afford even the slightest dissonance in their artificial harmony**"**

103

ARTUR SCHNABEL

born Lipnik, Austria
1882
died Axenstein
Switzerland
1951

"I am attracted only to music which I consider to be better than it can be performed**"**

WHEN THE ELDERLY LADY in the front row awoke with a start as the final ovation rang out, Schnabel leaned over to apologise: 'It was the applause, madame,' he whispered. 'I played as softly as I could.' Born when Liszt was still a living legend, at a time when to be a pianist was to be a celebrity and showman, Schnabel was told he 'would never be a pianist, since he was a musician'. He dedicated his considerable skills to the interpretation of the great classical composers, notably Beethoven, Schubert and Mozart (whose sonatas he considered 'unique; they are too easy for children and too difficult for artists'). Such were his early gifts that, rather than receive conventional schooling, he was sent to Vienna, aged seven, for intensive piano tuition. He studied with a man who had studied with a man who had studied with Beethoven, and it was this composer above all whose spirit flowed through Schnabel's hands. He recorded all his piano sonatas and concertos, performing all 32 sonatas in Berlin in Beethoven's centenary year (1927), and again in 1932. People of the calibre of violinists Carl Flesch and Joseph Szigeti, and cellist Pablo Casals, formed ensembles with Schnabel. He also composed three symphonies, five string quartets, and more besides. He had developed legendary standards of teaching at the Berlin State Academy by the time the Nazis took power – when, being Jewish, he left the city that had been his home since 1900 and emigrated to the USA. At the point Germany lost him, he was at the height of his fame, in demand worldwide.

WLADYSLAW SZPILMAN

born Sosnowiec
Poland
1911
died Warsaw
Poland
2000

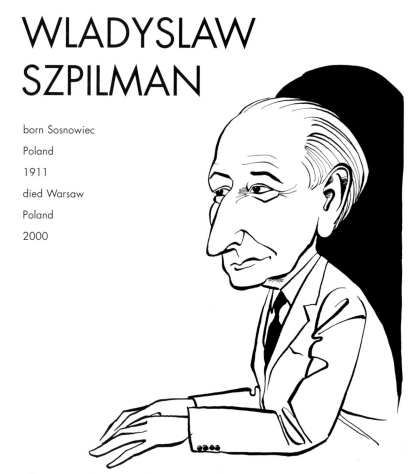

ONE OF SCHNABEL'S PUPILS in Berlin, who returned to his native Warsaw when Hitler took power, and played the piano on Polish Radio. On the day war closed down the broadcasting station, he was giving a Chopin recital. Miraculously, he survived the privations of the ghetto, the wholesale removal of the Jews to deathcamps, the destruction of Warsaw and the crushing of the uprising, to play Chopin again (the *Nocturne in C#minor*) when Polish Radio resumed transmission in 1945. He had played that piece on one occasion in the meantime: to a concerned German officer, Wilm Hosenfeld, who, finding him hiding and starving, saved him by bringing food, an eiderdown and an overcoat. Immediately after the war Szpilman wrote his personal story of survival, ***Death of a City***, but found publication suppressed by the Communist regime. So high was anti-German feeling that he felt it wise to portray his German benefactor as an Austrian. Many years passed before it was published properly in Germany, and then in England (1999) as ***The Pianist***, with added extracts from the despairing diary of Hosenfeld. Roman Polanski — who identified with the young man in the ghetto, surviving while his family were bundled into cattle trucks — made it into an award-winning film.

Szpilman returned to work at Polish Radio until his retirement in 1963. He performed worldwide, and composed a considerable amount of music — before the war, in the ghetto, and afterwards, when the Communist regime required popular songs for the masses.

"The reality of the ghetto was all the worse just because it had the appearance of freedom. You could walk out into the street and maintain the illusion of being in a perfectly normal city"

105

WANDA LANDOWSKA

born Warsaw
Poland
1879
died Lakeville,
Connecticut, USA
1959

"I never practise; I always play"

'SKELETONS COPULATING on a corrugated tin roof' was Thomas Beecham's verdict on harpsichord music. François Couperin, in 1713, admitted he would feel grateful to anyone who 'by the exercise of infinite art supported by fine taste, contrive to render this instrument capable of expression'. He had to wait a few centuries, but Wanda Landowska did Couperin proud. She did Rameau and Bach proud too – both were under-appreciated in the early years of the 20th century – and her contemporary, Poulenc, who wrote *Concerto Champetre* for her in 1928. Single-handedly, she led the revival of 20th-century interest in this, the staple instrument of the 17th and 18th centuries, which had been eclipsed by the piano, with its softer/louder flexibility. Her renderings remain definitive, both for musicality and scholarly understanding. She believed that 'the most beautiful thing in the world is, precisely, the conjunction of learning and inspiration'; wherever she was touring, she was always popping into libraries to peruse and copy out scores. From 1927, her home in the Parisian suburb of Saint-Leu became a centre for the study and performance of early music. When, being Jewish, she had to abandon it and flee south in 1940, her collection of old instruments and library of about 10,000 volumes and manuscripts were thoroughly looted by the Nazis. With help from Varian Fry she escaped to the USA, arriving on the day of the Pearl Harbor attack. After internment on Ellis Island, among crowds of bewildered Japanese, she was soon playing Bach's *Goldberg Variations* to the New World.

ALEXANDER ZEMLINSKY

ZEMLINSKY FELL DOWN A GAP between Romanticism and Modernism and got forgotten for decades. But his several operas and many songs, steeped in a rich, late-Romantic decadence, are better than the neglect would suggest. As an inspiring conductor, he transformed the Prague Opera House into a top venue, giving 35 performances of Mahler's symphonies with the Czech Philharmonic — yet nothing of his own work. As a teacher, he was revered by pupils such as Korngold and Webern; and Schoenberg — who married his sister — wrote that he owed him almost everything he knew about composing. Another pupil, Alma Mahler, with whom he was unlucky enough to fall passionately in love in the brief period she was trying to be chaste, called him 'dreadfully ugly ... yet I find him quite enthralling'.

He was a Sephardic Jew who, like many Viennese, converted to Christianity for his career's sake. When the Nazis came to power he was working with Klemperer in Berlin's Kroll Opera House. He fled back to Vienna, then emigrated to the USA, where, finding it impossible to master English, he gave up composing and died in obscurity.

born Vienna
Austria
1871
died Larchmont
USA
1942

"I lack what it takes to get to the very top. In this throng it is not enough to have elbows – you need to know how to use them"

born Hamburg
Germany 1903
died London
England 1996

BERTHOLD GOLDSCHMIDT

BRUNO WALTER

IN 1951 THE FESTIVAL OF BRITAIN invited entries — to be made pseudonymously — for a music competition. The organisers were mortified to find that two of the winning pieces had been written by foreigners: not at all in the spirit of the festival! And though performance was a promised part of the prize, neither piece was to see light of day until, in 1988, **Beatrice Cenci** by Berthold Goldschmidt was performed as part of an extraordinary revival of interest in a talented refugee who had the luck to live long enough, in his two-room North London flat, to witness it.

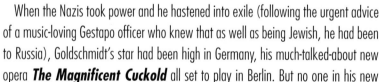

When the Nazis took power and he hastened into exile (following the urgent advice of a music-loving Gestapo officer who knew that as well as being Jewish, he had been to Russia), Goldschmidt's star had been high in Germany, his much-talked-about new opera **The Magnificent Cuckold** all set to play in Berlin. But no one in his new homeland wanted his composing, so in 1959 he stopped doing it. His gifts were used in other ways: conducting, teaching, voice coaching. He helped Derek Cooke prepare the 'performing version' of Mahler's unfinished Tenth Symphony and conducted its premiere.

"Berlin was always a liberal town. The Nazis came from nowhere**"**

Then, in his 80s, his adopted country discovered him, closely followed by the rest of the world. CDs appeared, and **The Magnificent Cuckold** was played in Berlin at last, 61 years late.

108

AT THE HEIGHT OF HIS CAREER, just back from a successful tour of the USA in March 1933, this much-loved and respected German conductor was informed that if he fulfilled his next scheduled engagements at Leipzig's Gewandhaus and Berlin's Philharmonic Hall, public order could not be guaranteed. 'Certain difficulties' might occur, meaning orchestrated Nazi violence. Despite his revered status, despite having discarded his giveaway birth-name (Schlesinger), he was, after all, a Jew. His place on the Berlin podium was taken at short notice by Richard Strauss, a musician at the top of Hitler's approved list. Strauss has been called politically naïve, an anti-Semite, a Nazi, and many other things, but his fatal flaw was probably an overweening sense of self-importance. He saw himself as the last mountain in a range that encompassed Mozart, Beethoven and Wagner and that would shortly give way to barren, flat land. This was not so far away from Hitler's view of music, so it is unsurprising that Strauss welcomed the rise of so cultured a leader. Goebbels appointed him president of the Reich Chamber of Music, and soon had him playing the Nazi tune.

born Berlin
Germany 1876
died Beverly Hills
USA 1962

Meanwhile, Bruno Walter decamped to Austria, where he had learned his trade as Mahler's conducting apprentice, directing the premiere of his Ninth Symphony in 1912. His welcome in Vienna ended with the *Anschluss* in 1938, so he settled in the USA, rounding off what was, Nazi persecution apart, a thoroughly successful career.

Posterity gives Mahler, rather than Strauss, a place in that lofty mountain range; his shadow touched composers throughout the 20th century. Walter was the keeper of his flame: it was his mellifluous recordings that nurtured the flowering of Mahler's reputation in the 1960s. Today he seems a safe sort of interpreter, a 19th-century romantic conservative at heart, glossing over the ironic tensions, restlessness and angst that others have revealed in Mahler's music. He hated jazz and disliked the discomforts of atonalism. Admirers called his style serene, others called it sentimental. Although he was universally beloved and respected as a conductor, and was an ostensibly polite and benign man, both Schoenberg and Mahler's daughter Anna privately called him a pig. He showed little interest in encouraging younger musicians, and it seems he was mean with his money when he might have helped struggling fellow exiles.

"Music's wordless gospel proclaims in a universal language what the thirsting soul of man is seeking beyond this life**"**

109

OTTO KLEMPERER

born Breslau
Germany
1885
died Zürich
Switzerland
1973

AT SIX FOOT FOUR, A GIANT as both man and musician. Battered by adversities and clinical manic depression, his eventual status and achievement owe much to his indomitable willpower and the devotion of his daughter Lotte. He was another Mahler protégé, whose first break had come conducting the off-stage instruments in the Second (*Resurrection*) Symphony. He took over the Kroll, Berlin's third opera house, and turned it, in four seasons, into a cutting edge venue, performing the classics in innovatory settings as well as contemporary masterpieces by the likes of Schoenberg and Stravinsky. 'Klemperer's Kroll' became the world-famous and controversial centre of musical Berlin. It fell foul of Communist critics for the modernist sets that ignored realism, and incensed the Nazis, who saw their beloved Wagner performed in modern dress — their German culture perverted by a Jew. A month after Hitler took power, Klemperer celebrated the 50th anniversary of Wagner's death with *Tannhäuser*. Another month and the Kroll was closed, being converted into Hitler's headquarters. Klemperer left town, sobered by Brownshirt raids and attempts on his life. In the USA, his chances of settling into the musical establishment were wrecked by his erratic and erotic behaviour in the manic phases of his illness: Mahler's daughter Anna recalls being chased around a table and only managing to ward him off by asking him deflecting questions about the score of Bach's B-minor Mass. In 1939 he underwent an operation for a brain tumour, emerging with facial paralysis and a further deterioration in behaviour. He left his wife; got beaten up; arrested. And horse-whipped by the outraged husband of Elisabeth Schumann.

At the war's end he went to Budapest, was well received and began to recover somewhat. But Communist restrictions drove him back to the USA, where the authorities harassed him and delayed renewal of his passport. When he eventually got it, he flew to London, and there respect and fame were restored to him at last with the Philharmonia Orchestra, which he conducted, sitting down and with minimal movements, until his 88th year. His status in 20th-century music was ensured. He was a tough disciplinarian with an acidic wit and powerful musical memory, whose mastery could make manifest the architecture of a Beethoven or Mahler symphony. Everywhere players responded to his high standards, and idolised him however hard he worked them and however rarely he praised. Once, when an orchestra excelled itself in performance, he uttered a heartfelt 'Good!' The stunned players burst into applause, only to be halted by the maestro's raised hand. 'Not,' he frowned, '*that* good!'

"In my day, Furtwängler and Bruno Walter and Kleiber and I *hated* each other. It was more healthy"

110

GEORG SOLTI

born Budapest
Hungary
1912
died Antibes
France
1997

A CABBAGE, daubed with the words 'Solti must go', was thrown onto the Covent Garden stage one night. The dynamic, bombastic, blunt, strict, hard-working man, who they called 'the screaming skull', was music director of London's Royal Opera House from 1961 to 1971, and his demanding and tyrannical approach was wrenching it from easy-going ordinariness into the top league again. Newly knighted, he now had a settled home in Hampstead, after a lifetime of insecurity. He was the last of the great maestros, with 30 Grammy Awards in his 50-year recording legacy with Decca.

Hungarian nationalism and anti-Semitism caused his father to Germanise young György's given name to Georg and to change the family name from Stern. Solti's nomadic life began when, knowing that a Jew would never be allowed to conduct the Budapest Opera, he took a job in Germany. As Nazi violence increased in the run-up to the 1933 elections, he backtracked to Budapest, intending to return shortly, as soon as Nazism had died down. Instead, Hitler took power, and his troops marched into Austria on the same night that Solti at last got his chance to conduct at the Budapest Opera – the first unconverted Jew ever to do so. Hitler had no need to annex Hungary; anti-Jewish laws were already being obligingly tightened, and Solti was reduced to private coaching. In 1939 he sought help from Toscanini in Switzerland, and there received a telegram from his mother, warning: 'Don't come home.' When they met again, after the war, she was a broken woman from years of hiding in a cellar. Solti remained in Lucerne throughout the war, saved from internment by a music-loving police chief.

In 1946, he received a note instructing him to be at the German border crossing at Krenglingen on March 20th, when an American jeep would pick him up and he would be taken to the Bavarian State Opera: 'they desperately need a conductor'. With displaced conductors seeking posts all over the free world, this was in fact the only way for Solti, now 33, to resume his thwarted career. But he got stick for returning so soon to the country that had slaughtered his fellow Jews. His time conducting in the bombed-out opera houses of Munich and Frankfurt established his reputation, leading to appointments at the Vienna Philharmonic (with whom he produced the first recorded *Ring* cycle), Covent Garden and the Chicago Symphony Orchestra. Career highlights included the German premiere of Alban Berg's once-banned *Lulu* and the English premiere of Schoenberg's complex opera, *Moses and Aaron*. He died on holiday, aged 84, never having lost his thick Hungarian accent.

"Sometimes, I think, like Faust, I would have been prepared to make a pact with the devil and go to Hell with him in order to conduct"

112

113

ALMA ROSÉ

born Vienna
Austria
1906
died Auschwitz
Poland
1944

"If we don't play well, we'll go to the gas**"**

GAS CHAMBER MUSIC. Orchestras were not unusual in deathcamps: there were half a dozen formed from Auschwitz prisoners alone. One of these, made up of around 45 women, mostly Jewish, was conducted by Alma Rosé with an unsparing toughness reminiscent of her uncle, Gustav Mahler. Alma (named after her aunt) was not as good a violinist as her father, Arnold (founder of the Rosé Quartet), or her sometime husband, Vasa Prihoda. A beautiful daddy's girl in a famous family, she basked in comfort and celebrity right up until the *Anschluss* in 1938. So unimportant was their Jewish identity to them that the Rosés were staggered to find it was necessary to leave Austria for England. Arnold, summarily dismissed from his position as concertmaster of the Vienna Philharmonic, never worked properly again. Alma, pursuing employment, went to neutral Holland, was caught out by the Nazi invasion, and ended up in Dr Mengele's infamous 'medical experimentation' block in Auschwitz. She was ordered to direct the orchestra and it became her day-to-day salvation. In return for the grotesque ritual of accompanying, with jolly tunes and marches, the daily departure and return of slave labour and the selections of the gas victims, she and her players were allowed adequate food and some bedding, and not required to shave their heads or wear prison clothes.

Her death was, for Auschwitz, perverse. It probably came from food poisoning, and she was mourned by the guards – who had addressed her as 'Frau Alma' instead of by her number – and also by Dr Mengele.

COMEDIAN HARMONISTS

MELLIFLUOUS CLOSE HARMONY, precisely delivered by five debonair young men in bow ties and tails around a piano, with extra instruments impersonated vocally. Inspired by the British group The Revellers, they sang their own arrangements of everything from folksongs to Strauss waltzes. They could conjure up a jazz band – complete with a soulful muted trumpet solo – for Ellington's *Creole Love Call*,

Harry Frommermann
born Berlin, Germany
1906
died Bremen, Germany
1975

Roman Cycowski
born Lodz, Poland
1901
died Palm Springs, USA
1998

Erich A. Collin
born Berlin, Germany
1899
died Los Angeles, USA
1961

and a whole orchestra in Rossini's *Barber of Seville* overture. For a while, between 1928 and 1934, the Comedian Harmonists were megastars in Germany and abroad, with 62 recordings and 13 film appearances, as well as countless live concerts so popular that tickets were often already sold out before the adverts appeared. By 1932 they were performing at the extremely highbrow Berlin Philharmonie, signifying that they were no longer purveyors of 'entertainment' but of 'art'. This classification meant their considerable earnings would no longer be subject to entertainment tax.

Yet this huge celebrity was no protection from Nazi cultural policy. Their English name was condemned, and their music considered 'not virile enough for true German ears'. Like all musicians they had to apply for membership of the Reich Chamber of Music and prove the racial purity of their line-up. The group's founder, Harry Frommermann, was Jewish, as were Roman Cycowski and Erich Abraham Collin.

The Aryans, Robert Biberti, Ari Leschnikoff and Erwin Bootz, stayed in Germany, became the Meistersextett, and complied with the Reich Chamber of Music's demands that all non-German songs and all jazz-influenced music be excised from their programmes. The Jewish half of the group emigrated initially to Vienna, and became a touring group. Finding themselves most popular in Australia, they settled there in 1937, broadening their repertoire to include songs in many different languages and styles, and changing their name to Comedy Harmonists.

Touring the USA in 1940, they were disconcerted to find that the outbreak of war had aroused anti-German feeling. They were out of favour, yet unable to return to Australia because of submarine warfare.

On hearing of the murder of his father in the streets of Lodz, Roman Cycowski quit the group, which led to its disbandment; the Aryan contingent folded in Berlin at around the same time. Cycowski, whose best efforts had failed to save any of his Polish family, honoured his father's memory by becoming cantor for the Jewish community of Palm Springs, California.

from left: Erwin Bootz (piano), Roman Cycowski (baritone), Robert Biberti (bass), Erich Abraham Collin (2nd tenor), Harry Frommermann (3rd tenor), Ari Leschnikoff (1st tenor)

jazz

The official Nazi position was clear: jazz was banned. It was the music of subhumans. Even when its practitioners were not Negroes, they were, likely as not, Jewish: Benny Goodman, for example. The spontaneity and individuality of improvisation were not in the German spirit. A decree of conditions for licensing dance venues (c.1938) makes stern reading. Its list of forbidden practices includes 'ostentatious trills, double-stopping or ascendant glissandi, obtained in the Negro style by excessive vibrato, lip technique and/or shaking of the musical instrument'; 'long, drawn-out, exaggerated tonal emphasis on the second and fourth beats in 4/4 time'. Expressly forbidden (and officiously spelt out) was 'the adoption in Negro fashion of short motifs of exaggerated pitch and rhythm, repeated more than three times without interruption by a solo instrument (or soloist), or more than 16 times in succession without interruption by a group of instruments played by a band'. The use of washboards, or mutes 'that effect an imitation of a nasal sound', were banned as being primitive, as was 'imitating a throaty sound' on an instrument.

And yet, the rise of Nazism coincided with the golden years of swing; what had been the art form of an oppressed American minority came into flower as a mainstream popular idiom, ubiquitous and irresistible. When Jack Hylton's band played at the Berlin Press Ball in 1937, Goering and Goebbels were both to be seen dancing (no, not with each other). The jaunty caricature on the Degenerate Music Exhibition poster – a black saxophonist wearing top hat and earring and sporting a Star of David in his button-hole carnation – falls short of the nastiness that Nazi caricaturists normally infused into their propaganda portrayals.

Goebbels, though he personally disliked the 'terrible squawk' of this 'Americano nigger kike jungle music', at once set about exploiting its mass appeal by granting radio air time to Charlie and his Orchestra, for whom Karl Schwedler sang cover versions of the latest hits, rewritten with anti-Semitic or anti-Churchill lyrics. Such gems as:
You're Driving Me Crazy

Yes, the Germans are driving me crazy

I thought I had brains, but they shattered my planes

and *Bye Bye Blackbird*

I never cared for you before

Hong Kong, Burma, Singapore

Bye bye Empire…

ERNST KRENEK

born Vienna, Austria
1900
died Palm Springs
USA
1991

KRENEK HIT BIG-TIME SUCCESS in 1927 with a jazz opera **Jonny Spielt Auf (Johnny Strikes Up)** which was staged at 100 different places. At the Vienna performance, pamphlets proclaimed 'our opera house has fallen victim to an impudent Jewish-Negro conspiracy! Take to the streets and voice outrage!' Its rather idealised portrayal of US jazz culture, personified by the easy-living black fiddler Jonny, betrayed Krenek's personal American dream of a land free of the weight of tradition. Not surprisingly the Nazis ensured he was soon on his way there. He set sail in 1938, even as, in the opening speech at the Degenerate Music Exhibition, his opera **The Life of Orest** was being singled out as a 'thoroughly putrefied work'. He became a US citizen in 1945 and lived out a long and successful career.

He was a composing chameleon, who moved from being an atonal *enfant terrible* with his 1921 **First String Quartet** through Neoclassicism (after meeting Stravinsky), then, via Schubert and Mahler stages, to Serialism, jazz and electronics. So deep was his 1920s obsession with Mahler that he found himself married for a few months to the great man's daughter, Anna — the second of her five husbands. Her mother, Alma, entrusted him with editing the sketches of Mahler's unfinished Tenth Symphony, and he made a performing version of two movements (1923) which was only superseded by Derek Cooke's version in the 1970s. Alma called him an egocentric, and she knew a few.

"I have been striving for an ever-free and more incisive articulation of musical thought"

117

DJANGO REINHARDT

born Liberchies
Belgium
1910
died Samois-sur-Seine
France
1953

"I don't even know what a C is; I just play them**"**

A DOUBLE DEGENERATE: Django was a gypsy and a jazz guitarist. In France, the Nazis were eventually to herd over 30,000 gypsies into camps and deport them to the east, where around 18,000 were killed. Yet, when he heard in England that the war had started, Django Reinhardt dropped everything —

including wife and guitar — to get back to Paris. There he survived the occupation, indeed prospered, thanks to his growing fame and the fact that, degenerate or not, many of the occupying Germans had a sneaking love of jazz. One, Oberlieutenant Schultz-Köhn, took Django under his wing.

Django was a dancehall pro at 13 and made his recording debut at 14, on banjo. He became possibly Europe's greatest jazz musician, gifted with lucidity and intuition: a natural improviser. This, despite being illiterate, and suffering burns so badly in a caravan fire that two fingers on his left hand were permanently curled towards his palm. He doggedly reinvented his guitar technique while bedridden for 18 months after this accident (caused when a candle ignited celluloid flowers that his wife was making for sale). When he discovered jazz, it was love at first sight, and happy chance teamed him up with dapper violinist Stephane Grappelli. Along with two rhythm guitars and a double-bass — but no drums or wind — they formed the Quintet of the Hot Club of France, making hundreds of recordings. Duke Ellington arranged an American tour for him, climaxing at New York's Carnegie Hall — where Django, typically, turned up late, having found a friend in a bar. His swing-based music, with little of the blues in it, lost favour after the war, and though he tried electrification, and was enormously admired by the new bebop stars like Dizzy Gillespie, he spent his last years, before a brain haemorrhage carried him off, doing more fishing and painting than playing music.

JOSEPHINE BAKER

born St Louis, Missouri

USA

1906

died Paris

France

1974

THE MOST SUCCESSFUL BLACK woman of her time. She was born into material poverty in a culture rich with blues and ragtime, in a period when new dance steps were arriving weekly. She learned them all, quipping that she only took up dancing to keep warm. When, still a teenager, she arrived in Paris in 1925, it was a match made in heaven: she was welcomed in a city refreshingly free of racism, that was currently obsessed with the exoticism of all things Negro. Her uninhibited song and dance performances — often wearing no more than a few bananas, and sometimes accompanied by her pet leopard Chiquita — drew adoring audiences and roused the wrath of both the Nazis and the

"Art is an elastic sort of love"

Catholic Church ('who hounded me with a Christian hatred'). She renounced American citizenship in 1937; and, on her later visits there, caused trouble by insisting on playing only to unsegregated audiences and joining and addressing civil rights marches.

Uninhibited, unconformist, outrageous and — of course — primitive, subhuman and degenerate: she was certainly on Hitler's list, but her huge celebrity cautioned the Nazis to leave her alone. She worked for their downfall, carrying secret information (often written in invisible ink in the margins of sheet music) from country to country for the French Resistance. She was awarded the Croix de Guerre and Rosette of the Résistance, and when she died, a 21-gun salute and the Légion d'Honneur.

She had many lovers of both sexes, marrying six times (though sometimes only as a publicity stunt). But she wouldn't drop her bananas for just anybody, and one rejected lover killed himself at her feet.

Besides Chiquita, her pets included Ethel the chimp, Albert the pig, Kiki the snake, various cats and dogs, a goat, a parrot, parakeets and a fish. She also adopted around a dozen orphan children of varying ethnicity (her 'rainbow tribe'), living with them in her chateau. When financial recklessness led to this chateau being repossessed, her friend, Princess Grace, found her a villa near Monaco. 'I want to live in peace surrounded by children and animals,' she said, 'but if one of my children wanted to go onstage in the music hall, I would strangle it with my own two hands.'

7

Undesirable

film

& theatre

itler loved film. So did Goebbels; a love he extended to seducing actresses. He once gave his Führer a Christmas present of 48 movies, including 18 Mickey Mouse films. His own favourites included Eisenstein's *Battleship Potemkin* and Fritz Lang's *Die Nibelungen*, both of which he would recommend as models for aspiring film-makers. Privately, he also loved *Gone with the Wind* and admired Hollywood's achievements; publicly he condemned American and all other non-German cinema. By 1937 he had gained control of the film industry by gradual nationalisation, and all foreign competition was banned.

The years of the Weimar Republic were a golden age for German movies, with Berlin the European centre for making films whose worldwide success brought welcome foreign capital into the depressed economy. But, keen though they were on the industry's money-pulling power, the Nazis were keener still on purging cinema of degenerate elements. Any existing films in which Jewish actors could be seen were banned, and new films had to pass scrutiny at the script stage and on completion. Through the Reich Film Chamber Goebbels was able to guide movie themes and content. Anti-Semitism was stoked up in films like *Jew Süss* and, most infamously, *The Eternal Jew* (1940), in which images of wretched Jews in the Polish ghettoes were juxtaposed with scenes of plague-carrying rats. The Polish footage had been shot personally by Fritz Hippler: in 1933 he had been a student organiser in the book burnings, now he was Reich General Manager for Film. Scenes of kosher butchering were advertised as too disgusting to be seen by women, and the film was promoted as a documentary that would inform 'calmly and factually' about Jews in their 'original state' – as opposed to the more familiar and 'humanised' West European types.

Goebbels was quick to realise that feature films that preached were going to lose their congregation. The place for propaganda was in the newsreels, which were pumped out for both home and foreign consumption. Even as classy a feature film as *Triumph of the*

timeline

1939
- Germany invades Czechoslovakia, then Poland
- Britain and France declare war on Germany

1940
- Germany invades Belgium, Norway, Denmark, Holland and France; occupies Paris
- British troops evacuated from Dunkirk
- Battle of Britain begins
- Pétain takes control of unoccupied France and signs armistice with Hitler. Terms include surrender of all Jews

1941
- First gassings of Jews, at Chelmno deathcamp
- Germany attacks USSR
- Japan attacks Pearl Harbor. America enters war

1942
- 'Final Solution' discussed at Wannsee Conference
- Jews forbidden to have newspapers, pets, bicycles, typewriters, buy milk, meat or eggs, or use public transport

1943
- German troops surrender at Stalingrad
- Italy capitulates

1944
- Attempt to assassinate Hitler fails
- D–Day: Allies land in France; Paris liberated

1945
- Hitler commits suicide
- Goebbels commits suicide
- Germany surrenders unconditionally to Allies

Will (1934), with its glorious mythologising of Hitler, he viewed with caution, despite its success. Leni Riefenstahl, who directed this masterpiece, had learned a great deal about the power of atmosphere in her years as an actress in the peculiarly German genre of 'mountain films', in which intrepid Aryan heroes were pitted against awesome nature, combatants matched in glacial purity. This sort of thing seemed much subtler to Goebbels: films that through entertainment would reinforce the Aryan myth and encourage the qualities appropriate to life in the new Germany. Discipline, comradeship and self-sacrificial heroism were celebrated with a stress on the unimportance of the individual. Historical celebrities such as Frederick the Great and Joan of Arc were reinvented as Führer figures. There was a spate of war films – at a time few were being made in Britain – which helped to prepare the German public for the struggle to come.

Meanwhile, actors, directors, writers and technicians of both film and stage were draining out of Germany, mostly in the direction of Hollywood. They took the Golden Age with them.

German theatre in the period before Nazism was no less dynamic and creative than German film. Nineteenth-century naturalism, in which actors played out drama as if unaware of an audience – who just happened to be watching them from behind the 'fourth wall' of their set – was ripe for challenge, and German theatre had the iconoclasts to make the challenges. Artists like Kandinsky and Kokoschka, having subverted realistic painting, applied the same ideas of abstraction and expressionism to naturalistic theatre. Dadaists brought elements of shock and politicisation; Marxists wanted to broaden the accessibility of what they saw as a bourgeois art form to wider and different audiences, and then confront and educate them from the stage. Creative giants emerged – Max Reinhardt, Erwin Piscator, Bertolt Brecht – and began to change the face of theatre.

Then the Nazis brought the curtain down.

MAX REINHARDT

THE AGE OF THE DIRECTOR began with Max Reinhardt. Tireless and imaginative, he thought big – money, no object – and inspired the many collaborators he gathered around him. He was constantly experimenting with the latest theatre technology and the use of dramatic space in the many venues he operated in. He revolutionised lighting with his application of the newly available electricity to stagecraft, and was quick to employ any newly invented mechanical trick. 'Real mastery in the theatre,' he said, 'comes from unending curiosity.'

Born as Maximilian Goldmann, son of a Jewish merchant, he first gained notice as a young actor playing the parts of old men at Berlin's Deutsches Theater. In 1901 he co-founded a satirical cabaret which quickly became his experimental drama laboratory, and after his 1905 production of Shakespeare's **Midsummer Night's Dream** had made his reputation, he became the new director of the Deutsches Theater. Before long he had built it into Germany's most celebrated stage. But one theatre at a time was never enough for him: he took over the Kammerspiele next door – a much smaller space – then alternated productions between the two. He started a school of stagecraft and a touring company, and spearheaded the theatrical renaissance of Berlin up to and into World War I. After that he moved to Austria, where he bought a castle and, together with Richard Strauss and Hugo von Hofmannsthal, established the Salzburg Festival. In his lifetime, he managed 30 different theatres and companies. His broad vision, rooted in a deep understanding of theatre history, made him a supreme eclectic whose 500+ productions (maximum: 48 in a single year) convincingly tackled most theatrical styles. In particular, he subverted naturalism by developing a more expressive and emphatic dramatic style, and this vision influenced Expressionist theatre and film.

After the Nazis forcibly requisitioned his German theatres and his Austrian castle, he left for the USA. He staged **A Midsummer Night's Dream** at the Hollywood Bowl, then directed a film version (with unlimited budget) for Warner Brothers. He threw himself into an immense Biblical epic called **The Eternal Road** – intended as a defiant riposte to the Nazis' vilification of the Jews – with text by Franz Werfel and music by Kurt Weill. It was to be staged at the Manhattan Opera House, but that proved too small for Reinhardt's grandiose vision: seats and boxes had to be ripped out, at vast cost. The magnificent scale of the project stirred up New York, and much cash was raised at a celebrity fund-raising banquet, with Albert Einstein leading the exhortations. The opening night arrived at last and was a triumph, with critical acclaim for the poetic libretto, the acting of a cast of hundreds, the music, the singing, the dancing, the staging, the set — the whole concept. Well attended and much talked about, the show went bankrupt within six months.

born Baden
near Vienna, Austria
1873
died New York
USA
1943

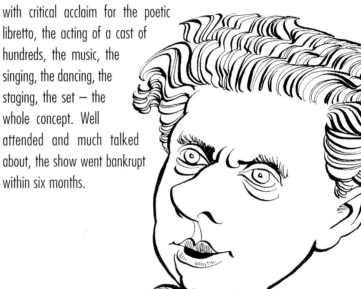

"I have spent my entire life on the meandering border between fantasy and reality, smuggling goods back and forth**"**

123

ERWIN PISCATOR

born Wetzlar
Germany
1893
died Starnberg
Germany
1966

A THIN, HIGH-PITCHED VOICE, according to Lotte Lenya, and not a physically impressive man, but he had great authority and persuasive fervour. His Berlin flat was luxurious, elegantly designed and furnished by Marcel Breuer, and Lenya describes him as 'looking faintly apologetic in all this Hollywood-style grandeur' — as any self-proclaimed Communist should.

After serving for two years as a soldier on the Ypres front, he began directing and acting in a theatre for fellow soldiers. The experience of World War I led him to Communism and Dadaism, and a desire to discard many theatrical conventions in order to confront the cultural assumptions of society — and in particular, those members of society who turned up for an evening's relaxed entertainment. 'Disrupting the spectacle', which often meant wrong-footing and offending the audience, was a radical departure from the 19th-century tradition of naturalism — which Piscator saw as being 'like bad photographs taken indiscriminately by bourgeois amateurs'.

With other Communists, he started the Proletarian Theatre, an ensemble built on the basis of shared revolutionary rather than artistic convictions. Amateurs performed alongside professionals, and the performances, on improvised stages in workers' clubs and beer halls, were packed out — not least because the unemployed got in free. Shows ended with the audience joining the actors in a rendering of the socialist anthem *L'Internationale*. The success of this project and its subsequent manifestations did not extend to making a profit, and in 1931 Piscator ended up in gaol for non-payment of tax.

Drawing on the inventive iconoclasm of Dada, he and his comrades brought many innovations into theatre. Besides much improvisation and audience participation, there were verbatim insertions of news reports and political documents, the projection of slides and footage, montages and mechanised sets. In this way, focus was directed away from interpersonal exchanges and onto the 'totality' of the work. The director's presence was now stronger than that of any actor. 'It is no longer the private, personal fate of the individual, but the times and the fate of the masses that are the heroic factors in the new drama,' he explained.

John Heartfield contributed a set for ***Tai Yang Awakes***, which extended from the stage around the auditorium walls. ***The Red Revue*** (commissioned for the 1925 election campaign of the Communist Party, and a model for countless agitprop reviews) began with a fight in the auditorium, from which protagonists

"Bourgeois art has nothing more to say. The whole of cultural life has become a mere formality**"**

emerged to argue points of view and comment on the stage action. ***The Adventures of the Good Soldier Schweik***, in which Brecht took part, featured treadmills so that soldiers could march steadily without leaving the stage, as well as cut-out caricatures by George Grosz and projected films and cartoons.

Piscator dreamed of 'a wholly new architecture, making the stage a play-machine, a wonder-world, an arena for battling ideas, perhaps even setting the audience on a turntable, dynamically bursting the static illusion of the present stage'. His friend Walter Gropius designed him a 2000-seat 'Total Theatre' along these lines, but no one ever found the money to build it.

He was filming in the Soviet Union when the Nazis come to power, and, as a Communist on Hitler's list, was unable to return to Germany. After a period in Paris, he emigrated to the USA in 1939 and founded the Dramatic Workshop in the New School of Social Research in New York. Marlon Brando, James Dean, Tony Curtis, Walter Matthau and Rod Steiger learned their trade there, but Piscator, aware he was unlikely to survive the McCarthy hearings, returned to Germany in 1951, leaving his wife behind to run the school. In 1962, he was appointed manager and director of Berlin's Freie Volksbühne theatre.

BERTOLT BRECHT

born Augsburg
Germany
1898
died East Berlin
East Germany
1956

'HOW D'YOU SPELL YOUR NAME?'

Frequently asked of German emigrés, this question was a wounding reminder to Brecht that in the USA he was no longer the iconic cultural figure he had become in Berlin. 'The intellectual isolation here is enormous,' he wrote. He had left Germany the day after the Reichstag fire, and reached America nearly eight years later with financial help from friends like Lion Feuchtwanger, after an odyssey that took in Switzerland, Denmark, Sweden, Finland and the USSR. America did not embrace him, and McCarthyism hurried him on his way after the war. Back in East Germany, though as much a Marxist as ever, and despite winning the Stalin Peace Prize in 1954, he found the comrades treated him no less suspiciously.

Lotte Lenya described him as 'skinny, with the frailness of a tough herring'. Always scruffy and unshaven, with dirty nails and rotten teeth, he was once excluded by security guards from a reception being given in his honour. He had a facial tic and a congenital heart condition, which led to a heart attack at the age of 12 and exemption from active service in World War I. He abandoned medical studies for the theatre, arriving in Berlin in 1924 to work for Max Reinhardt, with successes and a prestigious drama prize already under his belt. He had begun reading *Das Kapital* and found a keen interest in Marxist ideas stimulated by association with people like Walter Benjamin. From the start, his dramas showed nihilistic and anti-establishment tendencies. 'His emotions are rooted in primordial sounds,' wrote a critic, 'his hands uncover fragments of life.' Then came the smash hit that defined its epoch: **The Threepenny Opera** (1928), in which, said critic Herbert Ihering, 'morality is neither attacked nor negated but simply suspended'. On this platform of success, Brecht now built his theory of theatre.

A successful Brecht performance is easily recognised: the audience comes out alienated. Utterly unmoved but totally convinced. His idea was that while hearts were left cool, minds would be engaged in reflection and made aware of the need to overthrow the bourgeoisie; revolutionary action would duly follow. The audience is constantly reminded that this is a play, not reality; captions are written on placards, or projected, spelling out what is going on. The lighting designer switches the lights on full and sits back to watch the actors, who are

"The despairing hope of the theatre is to keep a hold on its public by constantly capitulating to its taste … But unless the public is seen in terms of the class struggle it must be rejected as the source of a new style"

126

specially trained to deliver the goods as unemotionally as possible, with occasional gestures and murmured asides to prove that they didn't especially relate to their characters, so neither should the audience. This was what Brecht termed 'epic' theatre – 'acting in quotation marks', breaking down the 'fourth wall' – as opposed to what he sneeringly termed 'culinary' theatre: what you and I might call a good night out.

But the public were constantly letting Brecht down. **The Threepenny Opera** was conceived as a biting satire of the bourgeois sentimental musical, filled with parodies of catchy songs. Yet the audience, far from being alienated, embraced it all at face value and went around humming *Mac the Knife* instead of manning the barricades. A year later, after the first two acts of **Happy End** had gone down delightfully with the first-night audience, leading actress Helene Weigel laid into them with a political diatribe in Act Three. This time they were well and truly alienated, but did they go straight out and start the revolution? They did not.

Progressing into more bluntly didactic plays, he lost his most gifted musical partner, Kurt Weill; and the public drifted away, finding the under-emotional dialogue wooden and the rebuff of their sympathies offensive. Yet, by bringing into drama approaches that were normal to Oriental and Ancient Greek theatre, Brecht had wrenched his art out of a 19th-century comfort zone in much the same way as Stravinsky had done to music. It prepared audiences for more challenging forms of theatre in the years to come.

127

HELENE WEIGEL

born Vienna
Austria
1900
died East Berlin
East Germany
1971

"Brecht was a very faithful man – unfortunately to too many women**"**

DESPITE HIS SMELLY FEET, Brecht had a great number of lovers, usually women. As a teenager he tended to keep around eight on the go at any one time, but settled down in maturity to a standard stable of three mistresses and a wife, plus hangers-on. Most of these lovers were collaborators, talented writers and designers in his ever-present retinue, and their contributions regularly found their way into Brecht productions, though more rarely into the list of credits.

The wife was Helene Weigel, daughter of a Galician toy seller. Lotte Lenya described her as 'small and slender, strong horse face … a toughie … a Yenta'. She studied from the age of 18 with Max Reinhardt and was already a well-known and established actress before she met Brecht; her film work included a part in Lang's **Metropolis**. She played leads in many of Brecht's plays and had some influence on his female characters. In **Mother Courage and Her Children**, the part of the mute Kattrin was written for Weigel initially, because she did not speak Swedish and the premiere was to be in Sweden. But it was the title character that Weigel subsequently made her own iconic part. 'Her way of playing Mother Courage was hard and angry,' Brecht wrote, adding hastily (lest we sympathise with the character), 'that is … she herself, the actress, was angry.' The archetypal 'epic' theatre performer, she co-directed the Berliner Ensemble with Brecht, and kept his flame burning for the rest of her life, performing her final Brecht role in **The Mother** at the age of 71.

LOTTE LENYA

born Vienna
Austria
1898
died New York
USA
1981

"I never took a singing lesson. Any Viennese can sing, you know? Really, it's in their blood**"**

KURT WEILL'S SOUL MATE: she married him twice. He gave her the big break she longed for, as Jenny in **The Threepenny Opera**, where her untrained singing voice set a style that has ever since evoked the sleazy jazz/cabaret decadence of early 1930s Berlin. And after his untimely death, she dedicated herself to promoting his musical reputation with recordings and tribute concerts.

Born Karoline Blamauer to poor Viennese parents, and abused by her father, she joined a circus and then became a teenage prostitute. An aunt took her to Zürich where she received ballet lessons and found acting opportunities, as well as love, with the theatre director Richard Révy. Taking lovers (of either sex) was a life-long proclivity, unrestrained by marriage. The men she actually married tended, after Weill died, to be homosexuals, alcoholics – or both.

Weill was Jewish, she was not. One reason for their temporary divorce may have been to recover his assets which would otherwise have been seized by the Nazis. Exiled in the USA, her acting career failed to revive until the 1960s, when she played Fräulein Schneider in the Broadway version of **Cabaret**, the title role in **Mother Courage**, and in films such as **The Roman Spring of Mrs Stone**, for which she was nominated for an Oscar. She tackled James Bond as the ruthless Soviet lesbian assassin, Rosa Klebb, in **From Russia With Love**. All the while her status as a legend grew, sustained by her engaging personality, her unmistakable voice 'one octave below laryngitis', and her longevity.

129

PETER LORRE

born Rózsahegy
Austria-Hungary
1904
died
Los Angeles
USA
1964

"All I do is talk in a nasal voice and make faces**"**

'YOU DESPISE ME, DON'T YOU?' asks Peter Lorre's character in **Casablanca**. 'If I gave you any thought, I probably would,' says Bogart. Peter Lorre excelled in such unsavoury parts: seedy, degraded individuals who nevertheless somehow engage our pity. Born László Löwenstein, he abandoned a good education (including tuition from Freud) at 17 for a theatrical career. Before long he was acting with Brecht in Berlin. Overnight movie success came when Fritz Lang used his chubby face and plaintive voice to give pathos, even dignity, to the fugitive child-killer in **M**. Goebbels was one of his greatest fans: one day, he amiably advised the actor that it would be good for his career if he toured abroad for a while. Lorre, who was Jewish, took heed, and was well away from Nazi Germany by the time footage from **M** reappeared in the 1940 anti-Semitic pseudo-documentary, *The Eternal Jew*, transmuting Lorre's child-molester's confession of base compulsions into a display of universal Jewish perversion.

A gall-bladder operation triggered a long-term morphine addiction that damaged Lorre's private life, though not, it seems, his acting. What did limit his performances was Hollywood's continual typecasting of him as murderers and psychos. He had one of the great movie faces: subtle shades of thought and feeling flickered across it, bulbous eyes and eyebrows working overtime. Two of the finest of his many films are **The Maltese Falcon** and Alfred Hitchcock's **The Man Who Knew Too Much**.

FRITZ LANG

born Vienna
Austria
1890
died Beverly Hills
USA
1976

"They all say I am dark and pessimistic ... however, I think that all my pictures are portraits of the time in which they were made"

IF HITLER HAD NOT EXISTED, observed one critic, Fritz Lang would have had to invent him on the screen. Influenced by Nietzsche and Freud, his films often explored the corrosive effects of seeking revenge, making a plea for compassion and forgiveness for sometimes quite despicable characters. In **M** he created a movie stereotype, the psychopathic serial killer; and again in **Metropolis**: a mad scientist, the precursor of Hollywood's Doctor Frankenstein. Despite its simplistic message, **Metropolis** was a cinema landmark, its art deco stylishness and visual splendours testimony to Lang's earlier training in art and architecture. It nearly bankrupted the UFA (the Weimar Republic state film studios), but this vision of an alienated society in a huge, futuristic city remains his monument.

Lang's original title for **M** – 'Murderers Among Us' – did not go down well with the Nazis. They were also unhappy with his film **The Last Will of Dr Mabuse**, in which the evil doctor spouted Nazi propaganda while staring madly from under sprawling eyebrows. Deciding it was time to harness him, Goebbels told Lang he was just the man to take charge of the Nazi film industry. Lang said he was honoured, packed his bags and left Germany that day. At least, that's what he said happened; he also said he reminded Goebbels that his devout Catholic mother was actually Jewish: Lang was a showman and worked hard on his personal myth. He moved to Hollywood and made dozens of films – some good, some bad – with stars like Spencer Tracy, Henry Fonda and Glenn Ford.

131

BILLY WILDER

born Sucha
Poland
1906
died Los Angeles
USA
2002

"I made
movies
when the
picture was
still more
important
than the
marketing
of it, more
important
than the
trailer**"**

BORN SAMUEL, BUT NICKNAMED
Billie after Buffalo Bill, Billie became Billy when he arrived in the US in 1934, having been offered screenplay work for a Hollywood film. In time he became one of the great directors, making films like **The Lost Weekend**, **Sunset Boulevard** and **The Seven Year Itch**. Actors and technicians had high respect for Billy's vision, judgement and restless energy. A meticulous planner, he had a critical ear, and defended the dialogue he wrote to the point that no actor was allowed to ad-lib. Psychological subtlety was a feature of his films. It also enabled him to work with people he didn't get along with (eg Raymond Chandler) or people who behaved impossibly (eg Marilyn Monroe), and still achieve what he aimed for. Even so, having cajoled two iconic performances out of the erratic Monroe, even the patient Wilder had had enough: 'I have discussed this with my doctor and my psychiatrist and my accountant, and they tell me I am too old and too rich to go through this again,' he said.

His father was a Galician Jew who moved his family to Vienna and changed his own first name from Hersch to the less Jewish Maximillian. Billie's first career was as a newspaper reporter. He once tried to interview Freud but was shown the door. He did better with the bandleader Paul Whiteman who, pleased with his article and keen for Billie to continue covering his tour, bought him a ticket to Berlin, the film capital of 1920s Europe. Besides jobs as a journalist and a dance partner for lonely ladies, he started writing film scripts: not such a hard job in those days of silent movies, but the beginning of a great career. After the Reichstag fire, he lost no time in selling his possessions and, with $1000 tucked in his hatband, left Germany for Paris. There he stayed in a hotel with other film industry exiles, including Peter Lorre, with whom he later shared a flat once they arrived in Los Angeles.

In Hollywood he soon learned that if you want to protect your script, you direct it yourself. His first hit as a director was the cynical *film noir* thriller **Double Indemnity**. In 1959 he made **Some Like It Hot**, just about the best comedy ever, with Tony Curtis and Jack Lemmon as cross-dressing musicians starring alongside a ukulele-strumming Marilyn Monroe.

After the war, he returned to Berlin as an adviser in the attempt to rebuild the German film industry, spending hours screening actors, directors and writers for their Nazi activity. There he learned that his mother and grandmother had died in Auschwitz, along with most of the Jewish community he had grown up with. He was asked to make a documentary out of Nazi footage of concentration camps. **The Death Mills** was slipped in as a 'B' movie for a German audience, but they were not yet ready to face such stark truths. 'The film started to run, and so did the audience,' said Wilder.

ERICH KORNGOLD

born Brünn (Brno)

Moravia

1897

died Hollywood

USA

1957

BEATING TIME WITH A SPOON at three, composing at six, called 'a genius' by Mahler at eight. He took lessons with Zemlinsky and, at 13, his second piano sonata was performed by Artur Schnabel. Still only 19, he saw his first two operas, **Der Ring des Polykrates** and **Violanta**, premiered as a double bill under Bruno Walter's baton. No, not Mozart — though Wolfgang was his second name — but Erich W. Korngold. Puccini observed, 'He has so much talent, he could easily give us half and still have enough left for himself.' When Korngold's next opera **The Dead City** premiered in 1920, it was recognised by all that an exceptional composer had arrived, albeit a very conservative one.

If time and taste had stood still, who knows what heights of fame and musical achievement he might have attained. But Korngold's musical soul was deeply, nostalgically romantic, and by the 1930s, there was only one place for such melodic lushness. He and Hollywood were made for each other. He arrived there in 1934 at the request of Max Reinhardt, who was directing a film version of **A Midsummer Night's Dream** for Jack Warner, with James Cagney as Bottom and Mickey Rooney as Puck. Who better to crown this epic with a glorious, Mendelssohn-based score than the *wunderkind* Korngold.

With his next score, for **Captain Blood** (1935), he established music as a primary element in a movie. Oscars followed, for the soundtracks of **Anthony Adverse** (1936) and **The Adventures of Robin Hood** (1938) — but he would still rather have been in Vienna writing operas and only the certainty of the fate meted out to Austrian Jews prevented him returning. His reluctance worked well for him businesswise: he got very good terms in his contract with Warner Brothers — including the option of rehashing his film music in future concert works — and began to make a lot of money.

Nevertheless, as soon as the war was over, he said goodbye to Hollywood and went back to Vienna, filled with hopes of finally coming of age in his home city. Only someone with his natural innocence, and the protection from reality proffered by spending the Hitler years cosseted in the Hollywood dream factory, could have been so unprepared for the changed world he found. The Viennese disparaged him both for his unfashionably romantic style and for having sold out to

"Music is music whether it is for the stage, rostrum or cinema. Form may change, the manner of writing may vary, but the composer needs to make no concessions whatever to what he conceives to be his own musical ideology**"**

films. Even worse, when he retraced his tracks back to Hollywood, he found his music out of fashion there too.

He was unlike other composers: from infancy, music seemed to be already stored in his head, to be poured out at will. The idea of artistic development or response to a prevalent aesthetic seemed irrelevant to him. 'You can't expect an apple tree to produce apricots,' he said, disarmingly. The man whom Viennese music-lovers in a 1928 newspaper poll had voted 'greatest living composer', alongside Schoenberg, ended his days rejected in his home country and forgotten in his adopted land. Yet, though he scored music for only 20 movies, he remains the undisputed father of film music.

ROMAN POLANSKI

A SURVIVOR IN MORE WAYS than one, as was proved by the awards showered on his 2003 film **The Pianist**. Polanski's triumph was hard earned; it came after some years in the critical doldrums, following self-exile from the USA to avoid arrest for having had sex with a 13-year-old. Basing the film on Wladyslaw Szpilman's account of survival in occupied Warsaw, he revisited his own ghosts, bore witness for those who were not allotted his luck, and celebrated the indestructability of art — in this case, music.

The film director responsible for such masterpieces as the scary classic **Rosemary's Baby** (1968) and the moody **Chinatown** (1974) was born in Paris to a Polish-Jewish family who, fatefully, moved to Krakow just in time for the Nazi invasion. Herded into the ghetto, they fell victim to events that have now been made familiar by the film *Schindler's List*. (Many years later Polanski was to turn down Spielberg's suggestion that he direct that film.) As the Jews were rounded up for extermination, Roman escaped through a hole cut by his father in the barbed wire fence, and survived the war thanks to kindness shown by Catholic peasants. His father also survived to be reunited with him, but his mother perished in the gas chambers.

After art college and the Polish State Film College in Lodz, he left for France and then Hollywood. His personal catalogue of grim experiences — in occupied Krakow he had been injured in an explosion and was used by German soldiers for idle target practice — continued in America when his actress wife, Sharon Tate, was brutally murdered by crazed disciples of Charles Manson. Polanski's artistic response was a bloody version of **Macbeth** (1971) and the poignant **Tess** (1979): Hardy's novel was the last book Sharon had read. Though his films inhabit a wide spectrum of genres, it is no surprise that darkness, alienation, gallows humour and pessimism are persistent features. An energetic and cultured man, he has also directed other people's works, including Berg's opera **Lulu** and Peter Shaffer's play **Amadeus** — in which he himself played the part of Mozart.

born Paris
France
1933

"Whenever I get happy, I always have a terrible feeling**"**

final act

That Bavarian prison governor back in 1924 couldn't have got it more wrong: the man who 'never made exceptional demands' had, by 1941, exercised his will over most of Europe, and was imposing his malign and genocidal programme on a whole civilisation. He was systematically wiping out a large ethnic group, not just within national frontiers but across a continent. At the same time he was taking on the military might of both the USA and the USSR.

The rest, as they say, is history. By 1945, Hitler's world was shrinking rapidly. Eventually he was as incarcerated as he had been in 1924, only now there was no remission. With him in his bunker was a rump of die-hards, the most devoted being his girlfriend, his dog and Goebbels. Outside, Russian soldiers and the hammer and sickle flag perched on the rubble of the Reichstag.

Hitler married Eva and they committed suicide together with the dog. That left Reich Chancellor Goebbels, as he now briefly was – the reward for years of unflagging sidekickery and spin-doctoring, the mad gleam of anti-Semitism still bright in his eyes – and the grimly determined Mrs Goebbels, plus their six children, all with names beginning with 'H'. She it was who probably gave them their nightcaps of cyanide, saving some for herself and her husband.

So ended Hitler's project; his own corpse joining the millions killed since he had come legitimately to power and started cleansing the German national body of its degeneracy. Despite the rhetoric and violence, Hitler was no revolutionary. Rather than consign the German past to a dustbin of history, he had wanted to restore it to his idea of purity by stripping it of the muck and corrosion that revolted his senses: everything from bolshevism and gypsies to atonal music and psychoanalysis; from mental disability to abstract art; from homosexuality to jazz. And Jewishness, above all. If only Hitler had become an architect and worked out his obsessions in a few grandiose monoliths.

Democracy should have prevented such twisted ideas from bearing such terrible fruit. But, as Goebbels put it, 'it will always remain one of democracy's best jokes that it provided its deadly enemies with the means by which it was destroyed'.

A lesson for us all.

GALICIA JEWISH MUSEUM

POSTSCRIPT

Here in Kraków, where the young Roman Polanski was one of just a lucky handful of surviving Jews, and with Auschwitz merely an hour's drive away, it is perhaps easier to relate to the 'degenerates' – both the geniuses and the ordinary, humble people – whom the Nazis found so 'undesirable'. And to appreciate the culture that flourished around them, with potential to enrich the world… until the Nazis came.

That the Galicia Jewish Museum co-published the original special edition of *Hitler's List* is highly appropriate for a venue dedicated to memorialising the decimation of Polish Jewry. This museum is the permanent home for a large collection of photographs that preserve the visual traces of a culture that Hitler had every intention of wiping out. During the complex years of Communism, while many memorials were erected at the sites of murder, all too many such remnants were left to rot. The museum was set up in 2004 with the aim of paying tribute to the former Jewish culture in Polish Galicia through the exhibition *Traces of Memory* which, along with an educational and events programme, recreates a Jewish presence for both Poles and international visitors in the heart of Jewish Kraków.

Chris Schwarz
Founder/Director, Galicia Jewish Museum, Kraków, Poland
www.galiciajewishmuseum.org

THANKS

Most of all to Sonja Wirwohl, whose academic work on Nazi culture and 'degeneracy' provided the original list and basic research, and Jacqueline Krendel for editorial nit-picking, comma-control and valued historical perspectives.

And to Chris Schwarz, director of the Galicia Jewish Museum, who first suggested the book.

ACKNOWLEDGEMENTS

A great number of books and websites were consulted in the making of this book. This is a selection of sources that were particularly helpful:

Bachrach, Susan D.
The Nazi Olympics: Berlin 1936

Barron, S.
Degenerate Art: The Fate of the Avant-garde in Nazi Germany

Bullock, Alan
Hitler: A Study in Tyranny

Cornwell, John
Hitler's Scientists: Science, War and the Devil's Pact

Eberle, Matthias
World War I and the Weimar Artists

Farneth, David (ed)
Lenya the Legend

Fischer, K.P.
Nazi Germany: A new history

Haffner, Sebastian
Defying Hitler: A Memoir

Kater, Michael
Composers of the Nazi Era

Laqueur, W.
Weimar 1918-1933

Lebrecht, Norman
The Maestro Myth

Lloyd, Ann
Movies of the Thirties

Magnusson, M. (ed)
Chambers Biographical Dictionary

Mahler Werfel, Alma
And the Bridge is Love

Medawar, J. & Pyke, D.
Hitler's Gift: Scientists Who Fled Nazi Germany

Reuth, Ralf Georg
Goebbels

Richter, Hans
Dada: Art and Anti-Art

Shirer, William L.
The Rise and Fall of the Third Reich

Snowman, Daniel
The Hitler Emigrés: The Cultural Impact on Britain of Refugees from Nazism

Spiegl, Fritz
Lives, Wives and Loves of the Great Composers

Taylor, James & Shaw, Warren
Penguin Dictionary of the Third Reich

Wulf, J.
Literatur und Dichtung/ Musik/ Theater und Film im Dritten Reich

Deutsches
Historisches Museum
www.dhm.de

www.exil-club.de

Lebrecht, Norman
La Scena Musicale (articles)
www.scena.org/columns/ lebrechtindex.htm

138